IT'S THE LAW --
A LAYPERSON'S GUIDE

IT'S THE LAW --
A LAYPERSON'S GUIDE

By

Brien A. Roche

Copyright © 2000 by Brien A. Roche
All rights reserved. No part of this book may be reproduced,
stored in a retrieval system, or transmitted by any means,
electronic, mechanical, photocopying, recording, or otherwise,
without written permission from the author.

ISBN 1-58500-849-4

1stBook – Rev. 5/31/00

About the Book

It's The Law – A Layperson's Guide is exactly as the title indicates: an overview of our legal system and legal principles that apply to the American Judicial System.

It is written in nontechnical language by an attorney with the objective of explaining to the layperson the sources of our law; i.e., what exactly constitutes the law, how our judicial system works and then a further explanation of specific areas of the law that may impact your daily life. The book is approximately 167 pages long. It is not specific to any particular state but rather is written in terms that would generally apply to most jurisdictions in the United States. It will hopefully give the reader a good overview of the nuts and bolts of our legal system and what to expect if you should become involved in a legal proceeding.

Foreword

There aren't many lawyer jokes that make me laugh but one that does bring a bit of a smile to my face is the cartoon that shows two lawyers sitting in the law library surrounded by hundreds of law books and one of the lawyers says to the other "It's frightening when you think we started out with just ten commandments."

The Ten Commandments are to be commended for their brevity. They are written either in the negative so as to prohibit certain types of behavior or written in terms of general moral precepts that no one could take issue with. Our American legal system, however, is designed to deal with much more mundane and complex day to day issues and further to give precise guidance to people not only as to what they cannot do but also what they can do. The moral law found in the Ten Commandments is written in terms of ideals of human behavior. Our secular law has to be more aware of the frailties and failures of our human existence and therefore for the most part cannot be written in terms of ideals or absolutes. What follows is designed to remove some of the mystery associated with our legal system and to put it into a more logical framework so that when someone tells you what the law is you at least have the analytical basis upon which to ask questions as to what law they are referring to.

It is important that you keep in mind that in reading the pages that follow that there is no way that something of this scope can address the law in all fifty states and as such the legal principles that are set forth here are written in general terms. The law that applies to any specific case may vary dramatically from one jurisdiction to another. I happen to be a practicing attorney in the Commonwealth of Virginia, Maryland and the District of Columbia. As such, many of the examples that I will give in this book will relate to this tri-state practice. That is not intended to suggest that the practice in these three states is necessarily representative of what goes on in the nation but it will give you specific insights as to how the system works in these states.

TABLE OF CONTENTS

Foreword ....*vii*
Table of Contents ....*ix*

Page No.

It's The Law xi

Chapter I   Sources of the Law

A. Constitutional Law 1
B. Statutory Law 6
C. Case Law 10
D. Administrative Law 21

Chapter II   Our Judicial System

A. Civil Justice in the State Court System....................27
B. Civil Justice in the Federal Court System................45
C. Criminal Justice in the State Court System 49
D. Criminal Justice in the Federal Court System 63
E. Juvenile Court..64
F. Traffic Court..65
G. What to Expect If Called As a Juror........................67
H. What to Expect If Called As a Witness 69

Chapter III   Areas of the Law
    That most Often Impact Your Life

A. Contracts..71
B. Torts 83
C. Domestic Relations..100
D. Criminal Law...108
E. Landlord Tenant 115
F. Estates 119
G. Taxes 125

H.	Real Estate	129
I.	Business Organization	138
J.	Bankruptcy	142
K.	Employment	146
L.	Worker's Compensation	151
M.	Insurance	157
N.	Eminent Domain	162
O.	Liens	164

Conclusion 167

IT'S THE LAW

You have probably heard people say on many occasions "It's the law". This is a very authoritative statement. But without some specification as to exactly what legal authority is being referred to, it may not mean much.

Our laws are derived from several different sources. Those sources are: (1) the U.S. and State Constitutions; (2) statutes or ordinances passed at the local, state or federal level; (3) case law that is published by either state or federal courts; (4) and administrative rules and regulations that are enacted by administrative agencies. The law may take any of the above forms. In order to understand whether the law found in any of those forms actually is binding in any given situation it is necessary to understand the scope of each form of law referenced above. What follows is an explanation of each of those different types of law; i.e., constitutional law, statutory law, case law and administrative law and how they impact our lives.

I. **SOURCES OF THE LAW**

A. **CONSTITUTIONAL LAW**

The Constitution that most people are familiar with is the U.S. Constitution. In addition to the U.S. Constitution, all fifty states have their own state constitution which to some extent is modeled after the U.S. Constitution but may vary from it. The state constitutions may give the people of that state greater rights than what the U.S. Constitution bestows upon them but it cannot restrict the rights guaranteed by the U.S. Constitution. The U.S. Constitution in that respect is supreme.

The U.S. Constitution is divided into seven articles and twenty seven amendments. The Constitution begins with the words "We, the people of the United States, in order to form a more perfect union, establish justice, insure domestic tranquility, provide for the common defense, promote the general welfare and secure the blessings of liberty to ourselves and our posterity, do ordain and establish this Constitution for the United States of America."

In essence the Constitution is simply a compact or an agreement of the people of that land to set forth certain basic rights of the people that cannot be taken away and to define what the powers are of the governmental authority that will rule the people. The Constitution truly is the foundation of our entire legal system. Some people would say that the rights we enjoy in this country are essentially natural rights and that the Constitution is simply a clarification of those rights and a limitation on the power of the government to infringe on those rights. Others may say that the Constitution itself is the actual source of the rights. That theoretical argument is probably of little significance to the reader. What is important to remember about the Constitution is that it does set forth the essential composition of our government and how it can interact with us as citizens.

Let me give you a quick test of your knowledge of constitutional law at this point. Suppose your next door neighbor breaks into your home looking for something that they think you may have stolen from them. The neighbor conducts a thorough and obviously unreasonable search of your premises without a warrant. Is that a constitutional violation? Hopefully the answer you gave to that question was no. The Constitution is a compact or contract between the people and the government. Constitutional violations can only be committed by the government or its representatives. As such, one citizen violating the rights of another citizen does not constitute a constitutional violation and has nothing to do with the constitution either at the federal level or the state level. What your neighbor has done is to violate state law and he can be charged with that state law violation and also could be sued civilly by you for trespassing and for damaging your property.

Article One of the U.S. Constitution sets forth the powers of the U.S. Congress and specifies that there shall be a House of Representatives and a Senate and defines how those members shall be elected and compensated. It also sets forth general powers and limitations of those legislative bodies. Article Two states that the executive power of the government shall be vested in the President and then defines the extent of that executive power, how the resident shall be elected and what his qualifications for office shall be. Article Three states that the judicial power of the United States shall be vested in the Supreme Court and such inferior courts as the Congress may establish. The model created here in the first three articles of the Constitution is a system of checks and balances. Each branch of government is considered to be equal and each one in different respects has the ability to check and to balance the others. For instance, the legislative branch has the authority to enact legislation. That legislation is then sent to the President who as the head of the executive branch can veto the legislation. The legislative branch then has to override that veto. If the law is passed and actually becomes law then it can be reviewed by the judicial branch for purposes of determining whether it is constitutional and also for purposes of interpreting the law. If the legislative branch for whatever reason doesn't like the interpretation imposed on the law by the judicial branch then it can amend the law so as to expressly state what interpretation should be applied to it.

Article Four of the U.S. Constitution defines the concept known as Full Faith and Credit which means that the public acts, records, and judicial proceedings of any one state shall be given full faith and credit in every other state in the union. That Article further defines the term known as "privileges and immunities" which means that the citizens of each state shall be entitled to all of the same privileges and immunities as the citizens of any other state. The privilege and immunities clause essentially precludes one state from granting certain privileges or immunities to its citizens that would not apply to citizens of other states. For instance, Minnesota could not grant Jesse "The Body" Ventura the sole right to conduct wrestling matches in that state to the exclusion of all persons who were not citizens of Minnesota. To allow such would be a violation of the "privileges and immunities" clause. Article Five provides for amendments to the Constitution. Article Six states that this Constitution and the laws of the United States made in pursuance of the U. S. Constitution shall be the supreme law of the land. What that means is that to the extent that there is any conflict between federal law and state law relating to an issue where the federal government has the right to legislate then that federal law will always be supreme. Article Seven of the U.S. Constitution simply provides that nine states are needed to ratify the Constitution before it becomes effective.

The first ten amendments to the Constitution are referred to as the Bill of Rights and they contain many of the most fundamental rights enjoyed by the American people. The First Amendment states that Congress has no authority to make any law respecting an establishment of religion or prohibiting the free exercise of religion. It further states that the Congress can do nothing to restrict freedom of speech or freedom of press or the right of the people to peaceably assemble and to petition the government. The Second Amendment deals with the right to bear arms but is written in the context of bearing arms as part of a well regulated militia. The Third Amendment states that the government cannot in time of peace quarter soldiers in a private home without the consent of the owner and in time of war may only do so in a manner prescribed by law.

The Fourth Amendment deals with unreasonable searches and expressly states that people shall be secure in their persons, houses and papers from unreasonable searches and seizures by governmental authorities. It further states that search warrants may be issued only upon a finding of probable cause. What that means is that there must be a determination made based upon substantial believable evidence that the person to be searched has committed a crime or the place to be searched contains evidence of a crime.

The Fifth Amendment defines the concept known as double jeopardy which means that a person cannot be tried twice for the same crime. That same Amendment further sets forth the right against self incrimination; i.e., that a person cannot be made to testify against himself. This Amendment also contains the foundation of the due process clause which states that a person cannot be deprived of life, liberty or property without due process of law. Due process is a critical concept to our entire legal system. It requires two things: (1) a person must be given notice of the charges or claims made against him and (2) further must be given an opportunity to answer those charges or claims before he can be deprived of his life, liberty or property.

The Sixth Amendment provides for the right to a speedy trial in a criminal proceeding and the right to a jury trial in a criminal proceeding. This Amendment further sets forth the right to confrontation in a criminal case meaning that a person accused of a crime has the right to confront the witness who is making the claim against him, has the right to compel witnesses in his favor to appear in court and give testimony, and further has the right to have a competent lawyer represent him in the defense of that criminal charge. The Seventh Amendment preserves the right to have a jury trial in certain civil cases.

The Eighth Amendment prohibits excessive bail and further disallows punishment that is deemed to be cruel and unusual. It is that Amendment that has been used to argue against capital punishment and other forms of punishment over the years. The Ninth Amendment states that the mere fact that certain rights are set forth in the Constitution does not mean that they are the only rights that people have. That is, whatever other rights the people otherwise had they still retain. The Tenth Amendment defines the initial thoughts of the framers of the Constitution to limit the power of the federal government by stating that those powers that are not delegated to the United States Government by the Constitution and which are not prohibited by the Constitution to the states are expressly reserved to the states or to the people. The point to be kept in mind here is that the initial framers of the Constitution viewed the U.S. Government as being a government of limited authority and whatever authority was not reposed in the United States Government rested with the states.

There are numerous other amendments that were passed over the years which are of significance. Perhaps the most important of those is the Fourteenth Amendment which was one of the post Civil War amendments ratified in 1868. That Amendment contained several clauses, the most important of which is the so called due process clause which expressly indicates that no state shall deprive any person of life, liberty or property without due process of law. You may recall that within the Fifth Amendment there is a due process clause. That due process clause, as is true of the first ten amendments, was deemed to be a restriction of federal power and not state power meaning that the federal government could not deprive any person of life, liberty or property without due process of law. That restriction however did not apply to the states until the enactment of the Fourteenth Amendment. Through the eventual interpretation of that due process clause contained within the Fourteenth Amendment most of the rights contained within the Bill of Rights were deemed to be no longer simply a restriction on federal power but are now deemed to be a restriction also on state power meaning that those rights contained within the Bill of Rights apply to citizens not only when dealing with the federal government but also now when dealing with the state governments.

The Fourteenth Amendment also contains what is known as the equal protection clause which states that governmental authority may not be used to deny any person equal protection of the laws. Over time that equal protection clause was interpreted to preclude governmental authority from denying black citizens the same protection of the laws as were accorded to white citizens. Other amendments of note are the Sixteenth Amendment which authorized the Congress to levy income taxes, the Eighteenth Amendment which enacted prohibition, the Nineteenth Amendment which granted women the right to vote and the Twenty Sixth Amendment which lowered the voting age to eighteen. The most important point to keep in mind in regards to the U.S. Constitution is that the document is simply a basic framework or foundation upon which our legislative, judicial and executive branches are built and which further defines certain basic rights that the people have that no governmental authority can take away. It is a document that is in many respects written in rather broad and general terms by the framers who wished to define the authority of government and then repose to the people all those rights that they did not bestow upon the government.

Aside from the U.S. Constitution, each state within the Union has a state constitution. Those state constitutions vary dramatically. The key point to remember in regards to the state constitution is that that document may bestow additional rights upon the citizens of that state but it cannot restrict the rights guaranteed under the terms of the U.S. Constitution.

Let me go back to the question that I asked at the beginning of this section involving the neighbor who breaks into your home. That type of conduct by one citizen in relation to another citizen does not involve any governmental activity and as such it has no constitutional dimension to it. That is, there is no issue of constitutional law relating to that type of conduct. The Constitution only comes into play when there is governmental conduct that is involved.

B. **STATUTORY LAW**

Statutory law essentially falls into three categories: federal statutory law; state statutory law and local statutory law.

The federal statutory law is found in the United States Code. The state statutory law is found in the state code enacted by the legislative body that governs that state. Local statutory law is found in local codes and ordinances. Those local codes may be county codes, city codes or town codes that are enacted by the local governing body.

A general principle that applies to this statutory scheme is a principle known as preemption. That is, where there is a conflict on a specific issue between federal statutory law and state statutory law then generally the federal law is going to preempt or supersede the state law. That same principle typically applies in regard to a conflict between state law and local law. That is, the local government cannot enact legislation that is contrary to the state statutory law. The logic behind this concept is that there has to be one entity that is supreme. For instance, in regards to taxation we would have an absurd situation if the Federal Government passed an income tax law which certain states decided that their citizens would not have to comply with. The American Civil War of course was fought in part over the issue of states rights; i.e., was the Federal Government going to be supreme or were the states going to be supreme on the issue of slavery?

The federal statutory laws are found in the United States Code. The copy of that code that most lawyers are familiar with using is what is referred to as the United States Code Annotated. The term annotated means that there are case notations following the code section from court cases that have interpreted or applied that particular statutory code section. Those annotations are frequently helpful in terms of interpreting what the true meaning is of that statutory code section.

Most state codes likewise are annotated and contain court decisions from both state and federal courts interpreting the various code sections.

Local codes tend not to be annotated simply because the local governments that publish the local codes do not have the financial resources to annotate their local codes and also because there tends not to be a great volume of case law interpreting local codes.

There is a shorthand abbreviation that is used for references to the United States Code. For instance, 28 USCS §1392 is a reference to Title 28 of the United States Code Section 1392.

The United States Code Annotated is a multi-volume code and as such in order to find that particular code reference you would go to Title 28. All of the titles are numbered sequentially. You would then look for Section 1392 within Title 28.

The state codes may have their own distinct numbering system. For instance, in regards to the Virginia Code, references to a code section would be to a specific numbered section such as Virginia Code Section 8.01-234. That is a reference to Title 8.01. Within that title you would then look for the code section designated as 234.

Local codes may be designated in a similar fashion.

The volume of legislation that has been passed by the United States Congress is in many respects mind boggling. There is Federal legislation on virtually every issue under the sun. It is important to keep in mind however that the Federal Government, even though it has its tentacles into virtually every aspect of our lives, is still a government of limited jurisdiction. You may recall from the section dealing with constitutional law that our founding fathers established the Federal Government as a government of limited authority with the understanding that whatever authority was not bestowed upon the Federal Government remained with the state governments. Obviously you would never guess that by looking at the volume of federal legislation. The most significant limitation that is seen upon the authority of the Federal Government to enact legislation is in the criminal sphere. For instance, the Federal Government has no authority to pass a statute that prohibits homicide in your private home on private property. The Federal Government does have the authority however to pass a law prohibiting homicide on a federal reservation, in a federal building or against a federal officer. As such most criminal prosecutions are initiated in the state courts under state law because the authority of the Federal Government to enact criminal law truly is somewhat limited. A fairly recent example of that dichotomy was found in the Rodney King case in Los Angeles where police officers were accused of beating a criminal suspect. Those police officers were first tried under state law and were acquitted; i.e., found not guilty. The Federal Government then stepped in and decided that those same police officers would be prosecuted under federal civil rights laws. The Federal Government had no authority to prosecute them for the simple crime of assault since the crime in question did not occur on federal territory, did not involve a federal official and did not involve a distinct federal interest as far as the assault only was concerned. The Federal Government however has passed laws that make it a crime for certain persons acting under the authority of state law to violate the civil rights of people. As such those police officers were prosecuted then in the federal court under that federal law. At first blush it would seem that this is a violation of the double jeopardy clause contained within the Fifth Amendment of the United States Constitution. It has been held however by the courts that that is not a double jeopardy violation since there are two separate sovereigns involved; i.e., the Federal Government and the state and in addition there are two separate offenses involved: one was an offense of assault under the state code and the other was a civil rights violation under the federal code.

It is in the criminal field that you see the authority of the Federal Government most clearly restricted in terms of its ability to enact legislation prohibiting certain types of crimes. That legislation must be related either to federal property, federal officials or involve some distinct federal interest. Typically a criminal offense occurring on a public street that is not on federal territory does not involve any federal interest and as such it is up to the state to prohibit that activity and then to prosecute it within the state court system.

The impact of local codes is most often seen in regards to housing, traffic and zoning issues. For instance if you want to build a home of a particular type on a specific piece of property that construction may have to meet certain zoning requirements in terms of height, size and proximity to the boundary line. In areas where zoning regulations apply, you probably would not be able to build a ten story home in a residential community with a building height limit of twenty five feet. Likewise, traffic laws frequently are set forth in local codes although those local traffic regulations have to be consistent with any state laws passed on those same issues. Again the issue of preemption applies there.

For instance, an absurd situation would exist if every locality were allowed to decide whether a green light meant go or stop.

C. **CASE LAW**

Case law very simply is the law as stated in specific cases decided by courts. That case law is in written form and generally contains a brief synopsis of the facts of the case, an analysis of the legal principles that apply and then a statement of the Court's decision or what is generally known as the holding of the case. The holding is the crux of the decision rendered by that court which then becomes law insofar as that court has jurisdiction or authority to interpret the law. Any language in the case decision other than the holding is surplus language or what may be referred to as "obiter dictum" or simply "dicta". The "dicta" within a court decision is not binding law but rather is simply utilized by that court to explain its rationale.

To fully understand the scope of case law and what effect it has upon our daily lives it is necessary to understand the structure of the court system.

In the United States there are two entirely separate and distinct court systems: the Federal Court system and the State Court system. Each state has its own court system which is entirely separate and entirely distinct from the other 49 states in the Union.

The Federal Court system however is somewhat integrated in that the Federal courts do not necessarily recognize state boundaries in terms of their authority.

The most important Federal court is the U.S. Supreme Court which sits in Washington, D.C. That court is composed of nine judges or justices who are nominated by the President and then approved by the Senate. The sitting justices are all attorneys and in fact most of them are former judges from lower courts who have been elevated to the U.S. Supreme Court. There is no requirement however that a U.S. Supreme Court Justice be an attorney.

The United States Supreme Court is a court of discretionary appeal. As a court of appeal it does not actually try cases but rather it simply reviews legal briefs as submitted by attorneys or litigants and then hears oral argument that are limited to an hour or two and then renders a written decision. The U.S. Supreme Court is not actually hearing from witnesses, is not hearing evidence and is not resolving factual disputes as might be done by a jury but rather is simply reviewing the record presented to it from the trial that occurred in the lower court and then determining whether or not there is a procedural, evidentiary or constitutional error that was committed at the trial court level. In defining the U.S. Supreme Court as a court of discretionary appeal that means that it exercises its discretion in deciding which cases it will hear. In order to have a case presented to the U.S. Supreme Court the party who is requesting the hearing must first file a petition. If that petition is denied then the case will not be heard by the U.S. Supreme Court. If that petition is granted then that means that the nine justices will hear the appeal and render a decision. Thousands of cases are appealed to the U.S. Supreme Court every year but only a very small percentage of them are actually heard by the U. S. Supreme Court.

The federal court system is essentially shaped like a pyramid. At the top of the pyramid is the U.S. Supreme Court. The U.S. Supreme Court is supreme and is final in the sense that it is the court of last resort. There is no higher court. Below the U.S. Supreme Court are eleven U.S. Circuit Courts of Appeals. The United States is divided into eleven federal circuits. (See the map on page 14A that follows). Within each of those circuits is a U.S. Circuit Court of Appeals which hears appeals from either the trial court below or from certain federal agencies which have a right of direct appeal to the U.S. Circuit Courts. These U.S. Circuit Courts are somewhat similar to the U.S. Supreme Court in that again they are simply courts of appeal. The U.S. Circuit Courts do not actually try cases in the sense that they do not hear evidence, the litigants do not testify in front of them and they do not typically resolve factual questions as would be done by a jury. The U.S. Courts of Appeal are simply reviewing briefs as submitted to them by the attorneys, then hearing oral argument of the attorneys that are very limited in their scope and then rendering a written decision or issuing an Order either affirming or overruling the decision from the trial court.

Below the U.S. Circuit Court of Appeals are the U.S. District Courts which are the trial courts within the federal system. The United States is divided into 91 federal districts. For instance in the state of Virginia there are two federal districts consisting of the Eastern District of Virginia and the Western District of Virginia. That is, the state of Virginia is divided in half into federal districts. In the United States District Court for the Eastern District of Virginia there are several different divisions that are part of that federal district. A division simply means that there is a courthouse located in that locality to serve the counties or cities within the proximity of that courthouse.

The United States District Courts are presided over by United States District judges who are nominated by the President to their position and then approved by the Senate. Also within the United States District Court there may be magistrates who are judicial officers who have the authority to hear certain types of cases assigned to them by the United States District Judge.

The United States District Court as a trial court is a court of limited jurisdiction meaning that it has only limited authority to hear certain types of cases. In the criminal area the United States District Courts can hear cases that involve any federal crime; i.e., a violation of federal law. For instance referring back to the Rodney King case, the police officers in that case were charged with a violation of federal civil rights law. They were tried in a United States District Court before a United States District judge with a jury that was composed of citizens within that United States District. A person who has committed a violation of state law typically could not be charged in the United States District Court with that crime.

It is important to make a clear distinction in your mind between criminal cases and civil cases. A criminal case is in essence a law suit brought by the government acting through a prosecutor against an individual who is accused of violating a criminal statute. For instance if you deface a federal building you may be charged with a federal crime in a federal courthouse. If on the other hand you punch your next door neighbor in the nose

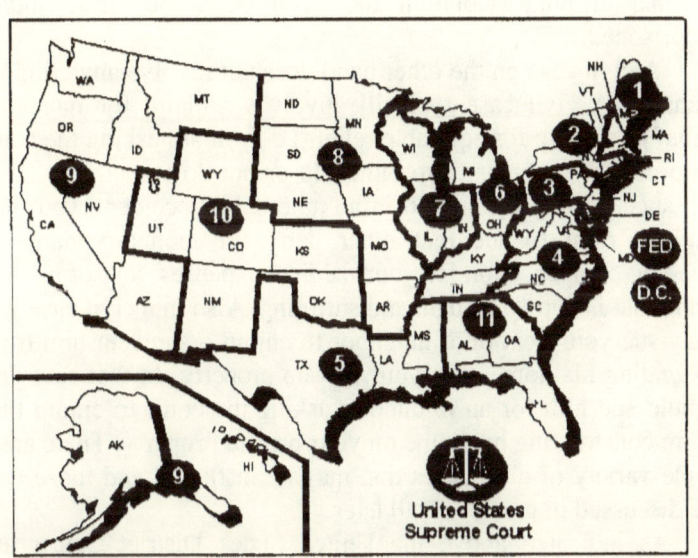

[Supreme Court | Federal Circuit | D.C. Circuit | First Circuit | Second Circuit | Third Circuit | Fourth Circuit | Fifth Circuit | Sixth Circuit | Seventh Circuit | Eighth Circuit | Ninth Circuit | Tenth Circuit | Eleventh Circuit]

on private property then you most likely would be charged with a violation of a state criminal statute and would be tried in state court before a state court judge and would have the right to have a jury present with that jury being drawn from the city, county or town where that court had jurisdiction. If you were found guilty of that criminal violation then you could be fined and/or imprisoned.

A civil case on the other hand does not involve any criminal penalty. A civil case typically involves a claim for monetary relief or a claim for equitable relief; i.e., you are asking the court to order the other party to either do or not do something. For instance, if you are injured in an automobile accident, you may have a right to sue that other party for monetary damages seeking compensation for your medical expenses, loss of income and what is known as pain and suffering. Also in a civil case you may sue your next door neighbor to enjoin or prevent him from extending his home onto your private property. In that case you would sue him for an injunction asking the court to enjoin him from constructing his home on your private property. There are a wide variety of civil cases that may be instituted and those will be discussed in greater detail later.

As indicated above the United States District Courts are courts of limited jurisdiction meaning that they can only hear federal criminal cases i.e., cases that involve a violation of federal statutory criminal law and they may only hear civil cases that involve either a question of federal civil law or which involve disputes between citizens of different states. This latter requirement dealing with citizens of different states is what is known as diversity jurisdiction in the federal courts. That is a citizen of the state of Connecticut may sue a citizen of the state of Mississippi in the United States District Court of Mississippi relating to an automobile accident that occurred in Ohio. Federal law requires not only that there be that diversity of citizenship but also that the amount sued for be at least $75,000.00. As such, if you were involved in an automobile accident in the state of Virginia while you were a citizen of Virginia and the other party likewise was a citizen of Virginia, you could not bring that suit in Federal Court because there is no diversity of citizenship. If, on the other hand the other party to the automobile accident was driving a United States Postal truck in the course of his duties then that case would be brought in the United States District Court under the Federal Tort Claims Act since it is a claim against the U.S. Government based on a federal statute.

The state court systems vary dramatically from state to state. Some states have a single trial court. Other states have what is referred to as a two-tier trial court system. For instance in the state of Virginia the lowest trial court is referred to as the General District Court. That court hears all criminal misdemeanor cases (a misdemeanor is a crime wherein the potential penalty is no more than one year in jail) and also can hear all civil cases wherein the amount claimed is less than $15,000.00. There are no juries in the General District Court. Any case that is heard in the General District Court may then be appealed to the Circuit Court where the party bringing the appeal is entitled to a new trial (referred to as a trial de novo). In the Circuit Court either party can request a jury trial. The Circuit Court is a court of general jurisdiction meaning that virtually any type of case can be brought within the circuit court.

Other states have only one trial court which is generally referred to as a court of general jurisdiction wherein all civil and criminal cases are initiated.

Many states also have what is referred to as an intermediate Court of Appeals. That intermediate Court of Appeals is essentially the equivalent of the United States Circuit Court of Appeals except that the state intermediate Court of Appeals only hears appeals from the state trial courts. These intermediate Courts of Appeal are like the United States Circuit Court of Appeals in that they will hear any case that is appealed to them. In some states such as Virginia those intermediate Courts of Appeal are courts of limited jurisdiction and may have authority to only hear certain types of cases.

The highest court in most states is referred to as the Supreme Court although some states may refer to their highest court by a different name. That high court may be a court of discretionary appeal meaning that they exercise discretion as to which cases they will hear much like the U.S. Supreme Court does. These courts of appeal, whether they be intermediate or supreme, are not actually trying cases but like the federal appellate courts are simply reviewing briefs and records submitted to them by the attorneys, then hearing oral argument and then finally making a decision which generally is in written form.

The case law that was referred to earlier in this chapter consists of the written decisions of the courts that I have referred to above. Typically trial courts do not generate case law. A trial court judge may issue a written opinion (decision) in a given case and that decision may even be printed in various law books. In that sense that decision by that trial court judge becomes case law but has very limited application. That is, another judge within that same court could decide a case identical to the first case but come up with an entirely different decision. That frequently does happen within trial courts; i.e., you have one judge who renders a decision that goes one way and then a different judge renders a decision on the same subject matter that goes the opposite way. Most judges and courts try to avoid that apparent inconsistency but that type of inconsistency can occur. What is important to keep in mind is that those decisions rendered by those trial judges are only binding in regards to that specific case and do not necessarily have any controlling effect upon any other trial judge within that trial court and do not have any controlling effect on any trial judge in any other trial court. Trial courts are the lowest tribunal and as such any written decisions rendered by trial court judges are of limited application. Many cases decided by trial courts are decided by juries. Juries do not render written decisions explaining their analysis of the case but rather they simply render a verdict. That verdict in a civil case would be either in favor of the plaintiff or in favor of the defendant. If the verdict is in favor of the plaintiff and there is an amount of money being sought by the plaintiff, then the jury would fix the amount of the monetary award; i.e., referred to as damages. If there is no jury deciding the case then the judge may enter a verdict or a Judgment Order fixing the amount of damages or granting one party the form of relief that is sought.

Case law for the most part comes from appellate courts. Those appellate courts may be intermediate appellate courts or they may be the high court of that state or court system. For instance, there is an abundance of case law rendered by the U.S. Circuit Courts of Appeal. There likewise is a wealth of decisions rendered by the United States Supreme Court.

Those decisions are contained within various bound volumes published by different law publishing companies. A written decision rendered by a United States District Court judge, if presented in written form, may be published in legal books known as the Federal Supplement or also referred to as Fed. Supp. A decision rendered by a United States District Court Judge may be referred to by the name of the parties, i.e., Jones v. Smith, 254 F. Supp. 1244 (E.D.Va. 1995). What that means is that decision rendered by that Federal court judge would be found in volume 254 of the Federal Supplement, page 1244, is a decision from a United States District Judge in the Eastern District of Virginia, and was rendered in 1995.

Decisions rendered by a United States Circuit Court of Appeals are typically found in law books known as the Federal Reporter which may be referred to as Fed2d. For instance, a decision rendered by the United States Circuit Court of Appeals for the Fourth Circuit would be reported at 254 F.2d 121 (4th Circ. 1995). That citation means that the decision rendered by the United States Court of Appeals for the Fourth Circuit, can be found in Volume 254 of the Fed 2nd Reporter at page 121, and is a decision rendered by the Fourth Circuit Court of Appeals in 1995.

Decisions from the United States Supreme Court may be reported in three different reporting systems all of which are published by different publishing houses. For instance a decision from the United States Supreme Court would frequently be referred to as Jones v. Smith 95 US 85, 125 S.Ct. 25, 92 L. Ed.125 (1995). That decision would be found in any one of those three volumes with the first volume being referred to as the United States Reporter, Volume 95, page 85. That same decision can also be found in the Supreme Court Reporter, at Volume 125, page 25 and would also be found in the Lawyer's Edition containing U.S. Supreme Court decisions at volume 92, page 125. The year refers to the year when the decision was rendered.

Written decisions rendered within the state court system are found in what I will refer to as regional reporters. The publishing house that is responsible for publishing state court decisions has essentially divided the United States into regions. For instance, Virginia is contained within the Southeast Region. As such a decision by the Virginia Supreme Court that is reported in written form could be found both in the State Reporter known as the Virginia Reports and also could be found in the regional reporter known as The Southeast Reporter. The decision of Jones v. Smith from the Supreme Court of Virginia discussed earlier would be reported under the same name with the following citation: 95 Va 85, 125 S.E.2d 25 (1995). The decision then would be found in volume 95 of the Virginia Reports at page 85 and would also be found in the regional reporter known as the Southeast Reporter at volume 125 page 25. Again, the year refers to the year when the decision was rendered.

Written decisions from trial courts at the state court level frequently are not published by any publishing house and as such to the extent they are available they may only be available within that local court house. Other states have adopted trial court reporting systems wherein certain written decisions that are presented to them may be published. In the state of Virginia there is a publication known as Circuit Court Opinions which consists essentially of written decisions made by circuit court judges in the state of Virginia. Those decisions however are only published if either the judge or one of the attorneys forwards that written decision to the publishing firm.

Courts either at the state or federal level are charged principally with resolving disputes that are presented to them and in that context render interpretations of state or federal statutes or state or federal constitutional provisions. Any decision rendered by a trial court judge is subject to being reviewed and potentially overturned by the appellate court that has appellate jurisdiction over that trial court. For instance, in the federal system any decision rendered by a United States District Court is subject to appeal to the United States Court of Appeals for that Circuit.

The United States District Court Judge may have rendered a written decision. That decision then can be reviewed by the judges in the United States Circuit Court for that circuit and those judges on the Circuit Court can either agree or disagree with the decision from the United States District Court. The decision rendered by the United States Court of Appeals likewise is then appealable to the United States Supreme Court. If the U.S. Supreme Court exercises its discretion and decides to hear the case that had previously been heard by the U.S. Court of Appeal, then the U.S. Supreme Court can either uphold or reverse that decision.

At the state court level the same procedure applies; i.e., any decision rendered by a trial court can be appealed to the appellate court that has jurisdiction and the appellate court can then either uphold or reverse the trial court decision. The high court within that state generally has the last word on those cases that are initially tried within that state although if the case involves an issue of federal law or a constitutional issue then the U.S. Supreme Court can decide to hear a case from the state court system.

In reviewing and analyzing case law from various courts, the import of that case law to some extent has to be evaluated based upon the status of the court that rendered the decision. For instance a decision rendered by a trial judge in the Suffolk County Circuit Court in Virginia may be of great interest nationwide but it is not binding on anyone other than the parties in that particular case in Suffolk County, Virginia. If that case however is appealed to the Virginia Court of Appeals and a written decision is rendered then that case law becomes binding over every person in Virginia as the law of Virginia. If that case is then appealed to the Virginia Supreme Court then the decision rendered by the Virginia Supreme Court becomes the law of Virginia and is binding upon all litigants in the Virginia State Court System. If that case involved a Constitutional or Federal issue then it may be further appealed to the U.S. Supreme Court in which event a decision by that Court becomes binding upon the entire Nation. In the Federal system a decision rendered by a United States District Judge typically is only binding upon the litigants in that case in that federal district. If that case however is appealed from the United States District Court to the United States Court of Appeals for that Circuit then the decision rendered by that United States Court of Appeals becomes binding upon all of the persons within that federal circuit. For instance the Fourth Circuit Court of Appeals includes the states of Virginia, West Virginia, Maryland, North Carolina and South Carolina. Any decision rendered by the United States Court of Appeals for the Fourth Circuit is binding upon all persons within that five state area. It is quite possible that the United States Circuit Court for the Eleventh Circuit could decide a case very similar to that and come up with an opposite conclusion. Typically where that conflict exists between circuits then that type of issue will be presented to the U.S. Supreme Court and the U.S. Supreme Court may then decide how to resolve the conflict between the Circuits.

In summary, the important things to remember in regards to case law are:

1. Within any written decision rendered by a court there normally are going to be one or more issues (questions) presented. The Court will generally provide a specific answer to that question or questions. Those answers are referred to as the holding of the case. That holding becomes the binding case law. There may be other statements made by the Court within that written decision but those other statements that do not constitute part of the holding are surplus and are not binding case law.
2. The particular application of case law is dependent upon the status of the court that is rendering the decision. A decision rendered by the U.S. Supreme Court on an issue involving the U.S. Constitution is binding upon every person in the United States. A decision rendered by the Virginia Supreme Court is binding however only upon persons in the state of Virginia.
3. The application of case law must further be

evaluated based upon the jurisdiction (jurisdiction in this sense refers to the authority of the Court to make its decision binding) of that court. Even though the U.S. Supreme Court is thought of as being "supreme" that does not mean that every decision it renders is binding upon every person in the United States. For instance, if the U.S. Supreme Court is solely deciding an issue of the Federal Rules of Evidence then that decision is binding only upon other cases that are tried within the federal court system. That decision has no binding effect upon the state court system or upon state court litigants. You have to look not only at the status of the court rendering the decision but also to the nature of the issue being decided and to what extent that court has the authority or jurisdiction to provide for a broad based application of that decision.

D. <u>ADMINISTRATIVE LAW</u>

Another facet of the law is what is referred to as administrative law. At both the state and federal level, there are administrative agencies. Most of those agencies are a part of the executive branch of government. As we saw in the section dealing with constitutional law, our government is divided into three branches: the Executive branch, the Judicial branch and the Legislative branch. The Executive branch at the federal level is headed by the President and at the state level by the Governor. The Judicial branch at the federal level is headed by the Chief Justice of the U.S. Supreme Court. At the state level, the Judicial branch is headed by the Chief Justice of the highest court of that state which in most instances is referred to as the Supreme Court although in some states it may be referred to as the Court of Appeals. Within the Legislative branch, there typically is no one person who is the head of that branch. At the Federal level, the legislature is bi-cameral meaning that it consists of two bodies. Those two bodies are the House of Representatives and the Senate. The Speaker of the House is the leader of that legislative body. The President Pro Tempore is the leader of the Senate. At the state level, there may be that same general type of organization within the legislative branch.

You may be asking yourself at this point, "What do the above comments have to do with administrative rules or regulations?" Although most administrative rules and regulations are promulgated by administrative agencies within the executive branch, there may be administrative agencies within the judicial branch or the legislative branch that could promulgate rules and regulations.

Let's start at the Federal level and look at some of the administrative agencies within the executive branch of government. The administrative agencies that most of us are probably familiar with are agencies such as the Food and Drug Administration, The Department of Justice, The Department of Commerce, The Department of Agriculture, and The Federal Communications Commission. Some of these Federal agencies are cabinet level agencies meaning that the heads of those agencies are members of the President's cabinet. Some of these administrative agencies are not cabinet level agencies and some of them may be considered to be independent agencies. For instance, The Federal Election Commission is an independent agency that has the specific responsibility of overseeing compliance with the Federal election laws by presidential candidates and other candidates at the national level. Another independent agency would be the Nuclear Regulatory Commission which is charged with the responsibility of overseeing the use of nuclear power in the non-military arena.

All of these agencies generally have the authority to issue regulations. These regulations in some instances may be referred to as rules. Although there is a technical distinction between a rule and a regulation, for purposes of our discussion here we are going to treat them as being one and the same. These administrative agencies are created by act of Congress and are given a specific purpose as set forth in the U.S. Code. The U.S. Code Section that created the agency also will set forth in general what the responsibilities are. In creating the agency, Congress, however, did not intend to be involved in the day to day administration of the agency and therefore delegates to the agency the authority to write and publish rules and regulations that will govern the conduct of that agency.

The rule making process consists of the agency publishing proposed rules; members of the public are then given the opportunity to comment on those rules; the rules then may be revised based upon that public comment and then final rules are enacted. The document where these rules are published is known as the Federal Register. The Federal Register is a publication put out by the Government Printing Office that contains all of the proposed and adopted rules/regulations of the federal agencies.

Within the legislative and judicial branches of government, there conceivably could also be administrative agencies that are in existence. For instance, the General Accounting Office is an independent administrative agency created by Congress and charged with investigating all matters related to the receipt, disbursement and use of public money. At the state level within the judicial branch of government, there may be an administrative agency known as the State Bar which is charged with the responsibility of administering and supervising the legal profession. Quite frequently, the State Bar is an administrative agency within the Judicial branch of government and therefore is subject to the control of the highest court of that state.

The regulations that are adopted by these administrative agencies have the effect of law. You may recall that we talked previously about statutory law. Statutory law is law that is created by a legislative body. At the Federal level, that legislative body would be the U.S. Congress. At the State level, the legislative body would be the state equivalent of the House of Representatives and Senate which together comprise the legislative body for that state. The legislative bodies that enact the statutory law endeavor to be as precise as possible in terms of writing the statutes. However, the statutes essentially by definition have to be somewhat general in many instances because the legislative body simply does not have the expertise or, in some cases, the time to enact statutes that deal with all of the nitty gritty issues that may arise within that subject area.

They delegate that function to the administrative agencies which do generally have the expertise and the time to publish regulations that are much more precise in terms of dealing with the nitty gritty issues that the agency confronts. The regulations published by the administrative agencies are designed to be an explanation and an elaboration of the statutes that the agency is charged with enforcing. Theoretically there should never be a situation where there is a conflict between what the statute says and what the regulations promulgated by the agency say. If there was such direct conflict, then the statute would be controlling. The regulations are designed to flesh out the statutory scheme. That is, you may think of the statutes as being the skeleton and the regulations as being the meat on the bones.

We had talked about the distinction between regulations and rules. Attorneys are very familiar with rules because generally rules are published by the courts and govern the procedure applicable to a lawsuit. For instance at the Federal level, there are Federal Rules of Civil Procedure, Federal Rules of Criminal Procedure, and Federal Rules of Evidence. At the State Court level, there may be equivalent types of rules.

These rules as referenced above are generally promulgated by the highest court of that jurisdiction and they are designed to provide some uniformity as to how a lawsuit proceeds.

Let us first talk about the Federal Rules of Civil Procedure. Those rules of civil procedure define what should be contained within a set of suit papers initiating a lawsuit (a complaint), define how a complaint is to be served, set forth what affirmative defenses may be raised by a defendant, set forth a variety of rules governing the discovery process and then set forth the procedures by which a judgment of a court may be reviewed by the trial court and then how that judgment may be enforced in terms of the plaintiff attempting to actually collect a money judgment against a defendant. The Federal Rules of Criminal Procedure govern how a defendant is to be dealt with in terms of the initial charging, his rights to be informed of the charge, what rights he may have in terms of discovery and further how the eventual trial will proceed.

Typically a circumstance would never arise wherein there is

any conflict between statutory law and rules promulgated by the court system. However, on occasion such a conflict does arise. When such a conflict does arise, the general principle is that the statute will control.

At the Federal level, all federal regulations are published within the Federal Register. They are further codified or contained within a document known as the Code of Federal Regulations (CFR). The CFR can be found in a law library and generally is organized in numerical fashion so as to correspond numerically to the extent possible with the statutory code sections that they are designed to interpret and expand upon.

These rules and regulations can be of critical importance. Suppose for instance you wanted to assert a claim against a motel owner because of carbon monoxide poisoning that occurred while you were in that motel. The type of claim that would be asserted would be a civil claim (law claim) for money damages based upon the negligence of that motel owner. There may however be regulations published by the state agency that control the motel/hotel industry that may set forth certain standards as to how motels are to maintain gas producing appliances so as to prevent carbon monoxide poisoning. Those state regulations published by that state agency could be extremely helpful in terms of pursuing a civil claim against that motel owner.

The legal profession itself is governed by rules and regulations published by their profession. Within every state there is an agency or entity that is responsible for publishing rules that govern the conduct of attorneys. Those rules of conduct are generally referred to as disciplinary rules. If an attorney violates a disciplinary rule then he may be disciplined by the State Bar and subjected to certain sanctions. For example, if you were represented by an attorney and found that the attorney had done something which you considered to be highly improper, you may want to look at the disciplinary rules to see if there is something set forth there that might govern the particular behavior in question.

This concludes the section dealing with the sources of the law. To fully understand what the law is you must know whether the law referred to is constitutional law, statutory law, case law or administrative law. In some respects, there is a certain pecking order or hierarchy that might be applied to those different aspects of the law. That is, if a particular activity is either allowed or disallowed under the Constitution, then no statutory law, case law, or administrative law can overturn that. That is not to say, however, that all constitutional rights are necessarily absolutes. For instance the people have a constitutional right to peaceably assemble but for purposes of maintaining public order, the government may require that you obtain a permit in order to conduct that peaceable assembly on public property. Simply because you want to peaceably assemble by calling a demonstration on Fifth Avenue in Manhattan does not mean that you have an absolute right to do that during the middle of rush hour. In that sense, your constitutional right to peaceably assemble has to some extent been restricted by state or local law that requires that you obtain a permit for that assembly. As such in looking at a legal issue or question, the general checklist of things that you would want to ask yourself are essentially the following:

1. Is there some constitutional provision that may be involved?
2. Is there any statutory law that may be controlling?
3. Is there any case law dealing with this issue and if so what court am I going to look at in terms of determining the source of that case law? If the issue is one that involves provisions of the U.S. Constitution, then the U.S. Supreme Court is the ultimate decision maker in regards to those questions and therefore I may want to look at case law from that court and case law from any of the lower federal courts. If the issue is simply one involving state statutory law, then I would want to look at case law from the highest court of that state.
4. Are there any administrative rules or regulations that may be applicable?

II. OUR JUDICIAL SYSTEM

We have previously discussed the general organization of state and federal courts. A federal judge may one day conduct a complex civil trial and the next day preside over a routine federal criminal case. There is no distinct demarcation between civil court and criminal court within the federal court system. Within the state courts there may however be a clear demarcation in some states. That is, there may be a specific court that is known as the criminal court wherein only criminal cases are heard. The important thing to keep in mind is that the civil system is entirely separate and distinct from the criminal system and indeed the rules that apply to one in many instances have no application whatsoever to the other. What follows is an explanation of civil justice in both the state court and the federal court system and then an explanation of the criminal justice process in both the state court and federal court system.

A. CIVIL JUSTICE IN THE STATE COURT SYSTEM

Within the civil justice system there are two types of claims that can be presented and resolved by the court: law claims and equity claims. A law claim is a claim for money damages. Money damages means that the plaintiff (the party bringing the suit) is requesting that a monetary judgment be awarded against the party who is being sued (the defendant). Another type of claim that can be litigated in the civil justice system is what is referred to as an equitable claim or an equity claim or it may also be referred to as a chancery claim. Those terms are all synonymous. Equitable claims are claims wherein the party bringing the suit is not necessarily asking for judgment for a monetary amount but is asking the court to direct the other party to either do something or not to do something.

A law claim might arise from an automobile accident where one party is injured and claims that injury is due to the fault of the other driver. The lawsuit may be filed requesting the court to award a monetary amount against the other party that is accused of being at fault. An equitable claim might arise when one neighbor is seeking to enjoin or prevent another neighbor from building an extension of their home onto the first neighbor's property. To prevent that type of encroachment, a lawsuit would be filed requesting an injunction to prevent that intrusion onto the property. If the court granted that request, then an injunction would be issued preventing that type of activity.

Within the civil justice system, there may be several divisions or offices of the Court dealing with different types of issues. For instance, there may be a landlord tenant division, a small claims division, a domestic relations division, a probate division and a tax division. Each of those divisions deals with the types of claims associated with their name. For instance the landlord tenant division will typically deal with landlord tenant disputes including evictions by landlords or complaints by tenants involving failure to comply with building code requirements. The small claims division may deal with any type of claim within the jurisdictional monetary limit that may be claimed in that division. It is not unusual for that jurisdictional limit to be $2,000.00 which means that no more than $2,000.00 can be awarded by the court in the small claims division. The small claims division is a type of People's Court wherein typically lawyers are not allowed and the strict rules of evidence may not apply. The domestic relations division deals with domestic matters including divorce, custody, alimony, child support and adoption. The probate division deals with estate matters and guardianship matters. Finally, within a civil court there may be a general civil division which would hear all claims other than the ones mentioned above.

Any person can walk into a courthouse in this land and file a lawsuit. The party bringing that lawsuit is referred to as the plaintiff. The party being sued is referred to as the defendant. The initial document filed with the Court to initiate a lawsuit may have different names depending upon the jurisdiction where you are filing. Typically the initial document filed with the Court to initiate a civil claim is referred to as a complaint. Within any such complaint, you can ask for either legal relief or equitable relief. If the claim being pursued is a legal claim then the damages being requested would consist of compensatory damages and perhaps punitive damages. Compensatory damages are damages that are designed to compensate the plaintiff for his or her injuries. To put that another way, compensatory damages are designed to make that person whole for the loss they have suffered as a result of the conduct of the defendant. Punitive damages on the other hand are designed to punish the defendant for egregious conduct. Punitive damages are rarely awarded and normally when they are awarded, they are carefully reviewed by the court to determine the appropriateness of the award.

Once a lawsuit has been properly filed by the filing of a complaint, then that complaint has to be served upon the defendant. It is served either by the local sheriff or may be served by a special process server or may be served by any other person authorized by law. That form of service typically is going to be personal service meaning that the complaint and the other court process (documents) issued by the Clerk of the Court upon the filing of the complaint have to be served in person on the defendant. Some states authorize what is referred to as substituted service meaning that the complaint may in some instances be delivered to a member of that defendant's household or in some cases may even be posted on the front door of the residence where the defendant is believed to live. If the defendant cannot be found through one of those means, then there may be other forms of substituted service allowed by state law consisting of service upon the Commissioner of the Department of Motor Vehicles in regards to an automobile accident and in some instances service upon the Secretary of State when the defendant is believed no longer to be living in that state. That however is governed by state law.

Once the lawsuit has been filed and the complaint has been properly served, then the defendant has a designated period in which to respond. Normally that period of time is anywhere from twenty (20) to thirty (30) days. The defendant may respond by filing a motion or by filing an answer. The different types of motions that may be filed by the defendant in response to the complaint would be motions raising issues of lack of jurisdiction, failure to properly state a claim, or certain other affirmative defenses. A motion based upon a lack of jurisdiction is a statement that this court does not have jurisdiction; i.e. the authority, to hear the claim. Another type of motion that may be filed is a motion to dismiss for failure to state a claim which means that the defendant is saying that even if everything stated in the complaint is true, that still does not constitute a basis for a lawsuit against this defendant. Other types of affirmative defenses that may be raised through a motion would be such defenses as the statute of limitations, res judicata, release, accord and satisfaction and several other such defenses. If a statute of limitations defense is raised then that means that the defendant is claiming that your suit was filed too late and is therefore barred by the statute of limitations. If a motion is filed based upon res judicata then that means that the defendant is claiming that this claim has already been adjudicated once and it cannot be litigated again. If the defendant raises the defense of release or accord and satisfaction then that means that there has been some sort of settlement reached in regards to the claim and therefore the reassertion of the claim is barred.

If no motions are filed within the time allowed after service of a complaint, then the defendant is to file an answer. That answer is supposed to respond to each of the numbered paragraphs of the complaint so that the plaintiff knows exactly what the issues are that are going to be contested. In addition, the defendant may be called upon to raise any affirmative defenses in that answer. An affirmative defense may be any of the defenses mentioned above that could be raised in the form of a motion or other such defenses that would constitute an automatic bar to the claim asserted.

Once that answer to the complaint has been filed, most civil claims allow for what is called discovery. Discovery is designed to allow each party to inquire of the other party as to what they know about the claim that has been asserted, who any relevant witnesses may be and the identity of any relevant documents. That discovery may come in several different forms. It may come in the form of written interrogatories consisting of written questions that either party may send to the other which then have to be answered in writing and under oath. The discovery may also consist of requests for documents and inspection meaning that the party issuing that request wishes to see documents in the possession of the other party or may wish to inspect certain things in the custody or control of the other party. In addition there may be requests for admissions which are written statements which the other party is required to either admit or deny. The purpose of requests for admissions is essentially to narrow the issues of contention in the case so that each party knows exactly what they are fighting over. There may also be depositions allowed. A deposition is an oral examination which is conducted in the presence of a court reporter. The purpose of a deposition is to have an opportunity to orally examine the other party or witnesses so that there are no surprises at trial. The overall purpose of this discovery process is to make sure that each side has an ample opportunity to discover the claims or defenses of the other party so that at the time of trial each party is fully aware of what the other party intends to present.

After the conclusion of the discovery process, there may be a pre-trial conference with a judge. The purpose of that pre-trial conference is to identify what the remaining issues are that need to be decided and to attempt to resolve any outstanding legal issues prior to the trial. In addition, some courts also conduct what are referred to as settlement conferences that may be conducted by neutral mediators which are designed simply to allow the parties to come together in an informal setting to discuss settlement with a neutral mediator. Those settlement discussions are generally confidential and if the case does not settle then anything said during those settlement conferences cannot be used against the other party.

If the case has not settled then it will be scheduled for trial. It may be tried either before a judge or a jury. Juries are picked from the general population of that city or county or jurisdiction where the court sits. Every state has different rules as to exactly how juries are chosen but typically they are chosen from the voter registration rolls and property ownership rolls of that jurisdiction. In some jurisdictions, they may also be drawn from the Department of Motor Vehicle rolls identifying persons who have driver's licenses.

If the case is to be tried before a jury, then the first stage in the jury trial is what is referred to as voir dire. Voir dire literally means "to speak truthfully". It is an opportunity wherein certain questions may be asked of the potential jurors to determine whether they know anything about the case, whether they know any of the parties, whether they have any interest in the outcome of the case or whether they may have any particular bias or prejudice for or against either party. That voir dire typically is conducted by the attorneys although in some courts it may be conducted by the judge. Once the voir dire is completed, then the parties have the opportunity to strike those jurors that they feel would not be receptive to their case. In addition, some jurors may be stricken for cause. For instance if a juror indicates that based upon what he has heard about the case he has already made up his mind then typically he is going to be stricken for cause because obviously he comes to the case with a predisposition.

Once a jury has been chosen, then the court will allow both parties to have opening statements. The purpose of that opening statement is to allow the attorneys to give the jury a road map of where the case is going to go. Opening statements are not intended to be argumentative but are intended to simply be a recitation of the facts that will be presented during the course of the trial.

Once the opening statements have been completed then the plaintiff will present his evidence first. That evidence comes in two forms: the presentation of testimony from witnesses and the presentation of documents or other tangible things for the jury to read and/or review. At the conclusion of all that evidence by the plaintiff, then the defendant has a right to make a motion to dismiss or to strike the plaintiff's case based upon any number of legal theories. This type of motion is a statement by the defendant saying that even if the plaintiff's evidence is to be believed it is not sufficient to justify a judgment being entered against the defendant. The Court normally will rule on that motion at that time. Typically that type of a motion is denied. If the motion is denied then the defendant has the right to present his evidence. At the conclusion of the presentation of all of the defense evidence then the defendant may renew his motion to strike or motion for a directed verdict as referred to above. In addition, the plaintiff, at that point, may make a motion to strike any defenses of the defendant and to request the Court to enter judgment against the defendant as a matter of law. That type of motion is a statement by the plaintiff that even if what the defendant says is true the defendant still has no bona fide defense to the claim and therefore there is nothing for the jury to decide.

It is important to keep in mind that the function of a jury is to hear evidence where there is a factual dispute and then to evaluate that evidence and then to render a decision based upon that evidence. If, however, there is no true factual dispute then there is nothing for a jury to decide and the Court (judge) will then make the decision.

At the conclusion of all of those motions the jury will be instructed by the Court as to what the law is in this case. Those instructions may be oral or they may be given to the jury in writing. The judge will read the instructions to the jury telling them what the law is that applies to the case. The jury will then be instructed to consider all the evidence, review the jury instructions and then render a verdict. Before they begin their deliberations, however, the jury will hear from the attorneys one more time in the form of closing argument. The purpose of that closing argument is to give the attorneys the opportunity to argue their respective positions on the case in order to persuade the jurors to vote in their favor.

The size of a jury may differ from jurisdiction to jurisdiction. The size of a jury in a civil case is anywhere from five to twelve people. The parties can agree to have a number of jurors less than that.

Any decision rendered by a jury normally is expected to be unanimous in a civil case. The jury reviewing the evidence is required to apply the principle that the plaintiff has the burden of proof. The plaintiff, being the one who is bringing the claim, has the burden of proving that case by what is referred to as the preponderance of the evidence or the greater weight of the evidence. If you were to think of a scale which is evenly balanced on each end and if a feather was to be placed on one side of that scale, then that feather weight would constitute a preponderance of the evidence. That is if the plaintiff tips the scales in his favor by so much as a feather weight, then the plaintiff has met his burden of proving the case by a preponderance of the evidence.

Sometimes people ask what does it mean to prove something. Something is proven by presenting evidence in support of it. I have previously indicated what constitutes evidence; i.e., testimony or documents or physical objects may all constitute evidence. Any one of those by themselves may be sufficient to prove something. One witness testifying that he saw you shoot your next door neighbor may be sufficient to convict you of murder even though you presented ten witnesses who said that you weren't even in the state on the date of the alleged murder.

Once a jury verdict is entered either party has a right to make post trial motions. Those post trial motions will typically come in the form of a motion for a new trial, a motion to decrease the size of a jury verdict or a motion in some instances to increase the size of the jury verdict. Judges are reluctant to disturb a jury verdict. The traditional thinking has been that once a jury has spoken then that statement is final. If, however, the jury obviously disregarded the instructions of the Court or returned a verdict that is obviously excessive or obviously inadequate then the Court has the authority to set aside that verdict and in some states to actually alter that verdict.

Either party, who feels as though they have not been dealt with fairly by the trial court, has a right to appeal that decision to the next highest court within that state court system. The particular structure of the different appellate courts has been previously discussed. An appeal is a very laborious process and in order to properly present an appeal the transcript of the trial proceeding may have to be prepared. That transcript is prepared by a court reporter. The court reporter expects to be paid for the preparation of that transcript. The mere preparation of that transcript frequently costs several thousands of dollars. In addition, the party bringing the appeal has to present a legal argument in the form of a brief or memorandum to the appellate court stating why the trial court decision is in error. The parties on appeal are not allowed to present new evidence. They are, instead, bound by the record created at the trial court level. Anything that was not properly presented or properly objected to at the trial court level is not going to be considered on appeal. An appeal is not an opportunity to re-try the case; it is simply an opportunity to request a higher court to review and correct an error made by the trial court and then to send that case back to the trial court for a new trial or in some instances actually reverse the trial court decision and to enter a new judgment.

Most courts have adopted rules of procedure and rules of evidence. Those rules of procedure may be contained to some extent in the state code in which event the procedural rules in essence become statutory law or they may actually be in a formal set of rules referred to as the rules of procedure. In the federal court system, there is a set of rules referred to as the Federal Rules of Civil Procedure. Those rules are very precise and they are all contained in one book. The Federal Rules of Civil Procedure were written by the Advisory Committee of the Judicial Conference of the United States which is a conference of federal judges and also lawyers who practice in the Federal Court System. Those rules are administrative rules in the sense that they are written by an administrative body, that is the U.S. Judicial Conference, and approved by the U.S. Supreme Court, but they are law as far as procedural matters in the federal court system. Many state courts have adopted similar sets of rules of civil procedure.

In addition there may be a set of rules referred to as the rules of evidence. In the federal court system, there is a formal set of rules referred to as the Federal Rules of Evidence that again have been written by the Judicial Conference. Those Federal Rules of Evidence apply in federal court.

At the state court level, many states have likewise adopted their own state rules of evidence. Those rules are designed to govern the admissibility of evidence in that state court system.

We have previously defined what evidence is: evidence technically is the presentation of testimony from witnesses and/or the presentation of documents or physical things for the jury to read, review or inspect. The rules of evidence govern how those things may be admitted into evidence. For something to be admitted into evidence technically means that the jury is allowed to hear it or see it. If it is not admitted into evidence, then the jury should not see it or hear it or if by chance they have heard or seen some of that evidence and the evidence is then not admitted, they will be instructed to disregard that evidence. The rules of evidence are designed to provide some degree of reliability to the evidence that is presented in the courtroom. These rules can become very complex.

The principle form by which evidence is presented is by simply putting a witness on the witness stand and having that witness respond to questions from the attorney who has called that witness. The testimony rendered by that witness is considered to be evidence. The jury may of course rely upon that evidence to decide the case. The testimony presented by one witness may be sufficient to convince a jury to rule in favor of the party that called that one witness even though the other party may have called ten witnesses who presented contrary testimony.

If you have ever been in a courtroom where multiple witnesses are potentially going to testify, you may recall the judge asking whether there is a request for a rule or more precisely whether or not there is a request for a rule on witnesses. The rule on witnesses essentially means that witnesses who have not testified should not be in the courtroom. That rule does not apply to the parties to the litigation. That is, the plaintiff and the defendant in a civil case both have a right to be present. In a criminal case, the defendant, of course, has a right to be present. Witnesses, however, who have not yet testified may be excluded from the courtroom until after they have testified. In addition, this rule on witnesses may be extended so as to prohibit anyone from talking to witnesses about what is going on in the courtroom until that witness has completed his testimony. A violation of that rule on witnesses may result in that witness being excluded from testifying. The purpose of this rule is to prevent one witness' testimony from being influenced by what another witness has said in the courtroom.

The party that calls a witness to testify is required to ask that witness non-leading questions. That form of examination, sometimes called direct examination is intended to allow the witness to testify rather than to have the attorney testify. If the attorney is allowed to ask leading questions, that is questions that suggest what the answer is within the content of the question, then in essence the attorney is testifying and not the witness. An example of a leading question would be "Isn't it true that you beat your wife?" That question by its very content suggests that the answer is yes, that the witness does beat his wife. That type of questioning is not allowed on direct examination.

The general purpose of direct examination of witnesses is to allow the party to call the witness to explain what he knows. If that witness provides testimony that needs further explanation, then of course the attorney can ask the witness to simply explain the answer. The purpose of cross examination on the other hand is to allow the adverse party, that is the party who has not called the witness, to try to pin that witness down. The witness typically is not allowed to explain his answers on cross examination. A skillful cross examiner typically will ask only questions in the form of "Isn't it true that...". That type of questioning is intended to illicit simply a yes or no answer and to not allow the witness to explain the answer. If the witness wishes to explain the answer or if the attorney who initially called the witness wishes to have the witness explain the answer, then that attorney on redirect examination, i.e., the examination that takes place after the cross examination, will have the opportunity to have the witness explain the answers that he may have given on cross examination. As such the general format by which questioning of witnesses is conducted is first by direct examination wherein non-leading questions are asked by the attorney calling the witness; second, by cross examination by opposing counsel through the use of leading questions; and then third the party that originally called the witness may conduct redirect examination consisting again of more non-leading questions allowing the witness to explain any answers that may have been given on cross examination.

Cross examination generally is limited by the scope of the direct examination. That is, on direct examination if the witness was only asked a very limited number of questions about limited issues then the cross examination is going to be limited to those issues. The cross examination may not go beyond the general scope of the direct examination.

Once a witness has been put on the witness stand, then he may be impeached. To impeach a witness means to contradict him in some manner or form or to undermine his credibility. A witness may be impeached by means of presenting to him contrary statements that he has made on prior occasions about the issue in controversy, by showing that he has some particular bias or prejudice against the other party or by attacking his character by showing that he has been previously convicted of a criminal offense constituting a felony or a crime if moral turpitude. A felony is a crime for which a person may be imprisoned for more than a year. A crime of moral turpitude is a crime that involves lying, cheating or stealing.

Normally in a civil case general character evidence is not admissible. The court in a civil action does not want to hear evidence about how good a person the defendant may be. That type of testimony however may be allowed in a criminal action as to the character and reputation of the defendant who has been accused of the crime.

The competency of a witness to testify may frequently become an issue. Generally any witness within the age of reason is considered to be competent provided that witness has not been declared incompetent by a court. A person is declared incompetent by a court if there has been a judicial determination by a court that that person is deficient in his mental capacities to the point where he cannot conduct his own personal affairs or business affairs and therefore needs to have someone else appointed as his guardian. If such a person has been declared incompetent, then he may not be able to testify. Frequently children may be challenged on the issue of competency. That is, a four year old child may not be competent to testify about what that child saw at a particular point in time. Normally it is a matter for the trial judge to determine whether that child is of sufficient sophistication to testify. Other issues of competency may arise in terms of taking of an oath. Some people maintain that they cannot take an oath because of their religious beliefs. Normally that is resolved by having the person affirm that they will tell the truth rather than having them state that they will tell the truth "so help me God".

In the course of litigation, it is not uncommon for one party to raise an objection based upon privilege. There are several different privileges that exist within the law. The husband/wife privilege generally precludes either spouse from testifying against the other based upon what they learned from the other spouse during the course of the marriage. If a husband tells his wife that he has just murdered the next door neighbor, then the wife may be precluded from repeating that statement in a court of law. She, however, is not precluded from calling the police to report the fact that the next door neighbor has been murdered. One of the privileges that is actually the foundation stone of our legal system is the attorney/client privilege. When a client retains an attorney, then anything that client says to the attorney is deemed to be privileged and cannot be repeated by the attorney without the consent of the client unless the communication involves proposed criminal activity. For instance, if a client tells the attorney that he is about to blow up the World Trade Center, can the attorney repeat that statement to anyone else? The attorney under the law of most states must advise the client of the possible legal consequences, urge the client not to commit the crime and advise the client that the attorney must reveal the client's intention to the authorities unless the client abandons the proposed criminal activity. A similar type of privilege exists in regard to the physician/patient relationship and the priest/penitent relationship. Some states also recognize other types of privileges wherein communications made by one person to another may not be divulged without the consent of the person to whom the privilege belongs. In the case of the attorney/client privilege, the privilege belongs to the client, and not to the attorney. If the client wishes to divulge those communications, then of course he may do so. The attorney, however, may not divulge those communications without the consent of the client unless the client has already divulged them on his own. Another privilege that exists is the Fifth Amendment privilege; i.e., the privilege against self incrimination. You may recall from our review of the Constitution that within the Fifth Amendment it is stated that a person cannot be forced to be a witness against himself. That is considered to be a privilege. Simply put a person who is a potential suspect in a criminal investigation cannot be forced to testify against himself.

We have previously talked about the fact that the plaintiff has the burden of proof in a civil case. There are different burdens that apply in different types of cases. In a civil case, as a general rule, the burden of proof is what is referred to as the preponderance of the evidence; i.e., the greater weight of the evidence. I had given the example previously of tipping the scales by a featherweight. If the plaintiff tips those scales by so much as a featherweight, then he has met his burden of proof based upon a preponderance of the evidence. In some civil claims, however, the burden of proof may be somewhat higher. In particular, in regards to fraud claims, the burden of proof is generally considered to be what is called clear and convincing evidence. That burden of proof or standard of proof is higher than simply a preponderance of the evidence. If you were to think of a preponderance of the evidence as being something more than fifty percent, then clear and convincing evidence would be a level of proof in the range of seventy five to perhaps as high as ninety percent. Another term that is used in cases is that of proof beyond a reasonable doubt. That is a level of proof that even goes beyond clear and convincing evidence and probably is more in the range of ninety percent, if in fact these different levels of proof can be quantified at all. It probably is unfair to try to ascribe numerical figures to any of these standards of proof since they really are not susceptible to numerical classification. These numerical classifications merely attempt to provide some illustration or demonstrative assistance in terms of understanding these different concepts.

Within the law of evidence, there are certain presumptions that may arise on occasion. A presumption is a recognition that if one particular fact is proved, then a second fact is inferred or assumed from the first fact. Let me give an example of that. If I prove that a child is under the age of seven, then a presumption arises that the child is incapable of negligence. That is, having proved first that the child was under seven, the court then recognizes a presumption that the child cannot be guilty of negligence. Another presumption of the same nature is that if a child is between the ages of seven and fourteen then that child is presumed to be incapable of negligence. This presumption is considered to be a rebuttable presumption. That is, if it can be shown that the child is of sufficient sophistication, intelligence and experience that he can understand the nature of his acts and is capable of committing a negligent act then the presumption may be rebutted. There are a number of presumptions that exist in the law. A person accused of a crime is presumed to be innocent. That presumption must be overcome by the government in terms of presenting their evidence of criminal behavior. If I am the person who holds the power of attorney for another individual and I profit from that relationship, then there is a presumption that my profiting from that relationship is fraudulent. The basis for that presumption is that I am the attorney in fact or hold a power of attorney for that individual and therefore control that person and have a great deal of power over that individual where I can manipulate the assets or activity of that individual. If I then am shown to have profited from that relationship in some manner, then that profit is generally going to be considered fraudulent; i.e., presumed to be fraudulent unless I can rebut that. Another presumption that may arise is a presumption of death from an absence of seven years. If a person disappears and is not seen from for a period of seven years, then there arises a presumption that the person is dead. Another presumption that is frequently referred to is the presumption of knowledge of the law. You as a citizen of this country are presumed to know the law. Obviously we all know that you cannot know all of the laws. Common sense should tell you that if you are about to engage in some behavior that is questionable, then you may need to check to see whether that behavior is illegal. If you then engage in that behavior, you cannot raise a defense that you did not know the law because the law says that you are presumed to know the law.

In terms of looking at the admissibility of evidence in the course of a court proceeding, the principle criteria of admissibility is that the evidence must be relevant. Relevance means that the evidence that is being offered tends to prove or disprove an issue in the case. If the issue in the case is whether you ran a red light then evidence that shows that that traffic light was not properly functioning at the time of the accident certainly is relevant and typically would be admissible. Likewise, evidence of the cycle of nearby traffic lights and your speed as you travel from a nearby intersection to the intersection in question may all be relevant as to whether or not the light was in fact red when you entered the intersection in question. All of those facts or evidence tend to prove or disprove whether you ran that red light and therefore are relevant.

Some evidence may be relevant but it is so highly prejudicial that the court determines that it should not be admitted. In tort claims, most courts have determined that evidence of insurance is not admissible because it is too prejudicial. That is, if a jury knew that a defendant was insured then jury verdicts may be higher simply because of that. In light of that, most courts have determined that evidence of a defendant being insured is not admissible even though it may be relevant. It may be relevant that a defendant at the scene made certain statements about his being insured; made certain statements after the accident to the claims adjuster who investigated the claim; or at the scene of the accident, made certain admissions as to how much insurance coverage he may have in order to cover the damages incurred. Although these statements may be relevant in the sense that they tend to prove or disprove the issue of whether he is at fault, the courts have determined that typically evidence of insurance in that context is too prejudicial and therefore not admissible.

Evidence in general terms can fall into two broad categories.

There is direct evidence and then there is circumstantial evidence. Direct evidence consists of a person testifying that "I saw the wolf attack the chicken coop". A second form of evidence is circumstantial evidence which may come in the form of a person looking at the chicken coop and then seeing a wolf's tracks around the chicken coop. Those tracks of the wolf are circumstantial evidence that the wolf was there and that he attacked the chickens.

Documents and physical objects are frequently offered as exhibits or as evidence at trial. The threshold inquiry in regards to any document or other physical object is whether it is authentic. A document or object is authentic if in fact it has been proven to be what it appears to be. If a Will is presented to the court as an exhibit and is offered as the Will of John Jones, then before that document can be entered into as evidence; i.e., shown to the jury, a witness will need to confirm that in fact it is the Will of John Jones and that the document bears his signature. That type of testimony establishes the authenticity of the document; i.e., simply that it is what it appears to be. From a common sense point of view, lay people in looking at that Will, may say that it has the name at the top indicating that it is the Last Will and Testament of John Jones, it bears the signature of John Jones, and the signature appears to be authentic. Based upon all of that, common sense would suggest that the document is in fact what it appears to be; i.e., the Last Will and Testament of John Jones. The court, however, normally requires more than simply that appearance of validity. Typically a witness will need to testify that the document is in fact the Last Will and Testament of John Jones and he may have to testify as to how he knows that is so. Once the authenticity of a document has been established, then there may be other objections that could be made as to that document. Any objections as to relevancy and privilege will have to be dealt with.

A more common objection, however, to a document may be simply that of it being hearsay. The hearsay objection may arise not only in regards to documentary evidence but also in regards to testimonial evidence; i.e., the testimony of witnesses. Hearsay in general is an out of court statement that is being offered for its truth value. If the plaintiff makes a statement at the scene of the accident saying that "I am at fault", is that hearsay? Again looking at the definition of hearsay as being an out of court statement that is offered for its truth value, then under that definition the statement would be hearsay. The statement was made out of court; i.e., at the accident scene and secondly it is being offered for its truth value; i.e., to prove that the plaintiff was at fault at the time of the accident because he said so. That type of statement technically is hearsay although the court may still admit it on the grounds of it being an exception to the hearsay rule because it is an admission of a party to this particular action, i.e., an admission of fault. The general purpose of the hearsay rule is to exclude types of evidence that may not be reliable. Another reason for the exclusion of hearsay evidence is because the presentation of hearsay evidence denies the other party the right to cross examine the person who is making the statement. If at the scene of an accident, a police officer makes a statement to the effect that the plaintiff was at fault for the accident, that statement is hearsay because it is an out of court statement and it is being offered for its truth value. If the police officer does not testify at trial, then obviously he cannot be cross examined about that statement therefore it would be unfair to allow either party to repeat that statement in court because the witness making the statement is not present to be cross examined about the statement. If, however, the police officer does testify at trial, then it is possible that under certain circumstances he may be confronted with that prior statement that he had made and asked to explain it.

As indicated above the general definition of hearsay is simply an out of court statement that is offered for its truth value. In general, hearsay evidence is not admissible but there are a number of exceptions to the hearsay rule. Those exceptions are very extensive and some people might say that the exceptions are so extensive that the rule now has no meaning.

We have probably all heard of so called experts who testify in either civil cases or criminal cases. The term expert has become somewhat maligned. An expert witness is simply a witness who has certain expertise in a particular area and the court has determined that the expert testimony may assist the jury in terms of understanding the issues of the case and therefore fairly deciding the issues. Expert testimony has been somewhat abused over the years in that it is presented in regards to issues that perhaps do not require expert testimony. The general rule of thumb for the admissibility of expert testimony is that it must relate to a subject matter that the jury might otherwise have difficulty understanding without the use of expert testimony to assist it in understanding the issue. In a medical malpractice case where there is an issue as to whether the surgery should have been conducted one way or another, then of course the jury needs to hear expert testimony from medical doctors as to how the surgery should have been conducted. The jury does not have the expertise to decide that issue on its own and therefore must hear from medical experts who will educate the jurors as to what the medical issues are and how the surgery either should have or should not have been conducted. It is then up to the jury to decide which of those experts they believe and to render a verdict based upon that. Some types of expert testimony have been ruled inadmissible by some courts. For instance, evidence of how a particular automobile accident may have occurred, in some jurisdictions, is considered to be inadmissible because that normally is considered to be something that is within the general confines of what a jury can understand and determine on its own without the aid of expert testimony. There is a tendency within the legal profession to offer expert testimony on as many issues as possible in order to bolster the claim or defense being asserted. Recently many courts have taken a somewhat dim view of that and have endeavored to restrict the admissibility of expert testimony on the theory that in many of these types of cases, the jury has sufficient expertise or common sense to understand the true issues and to resolve those issues without the assistance of expert testimony.

B. <u>CIVIL JUSTICE IN THE FEDERAL COURT SYSTEM</u>

The federal court system in many respects is quite different than the state court system. You will recall from what was said previously that the federal courts are courts of limited jurisdiction. On the other hand, the state courts are courts of general jurisdiction or, to put it another way, virtually of <u>unlimited</u> jurisdiction. The term jurisdiction in this sense refers to subject matter jurisdiction; i.e., the types of claims that the court has the authority to hear. There are some claims arising under federal law that can be asserted only in federal court but the general rule is that virtually any type of civil claim can be brought in the state court system. That is not true of the federal court system. In order to bring a civil claim in the federal court, there are certain subject matter jurisdictional requirements that have to be met. To put that another way, there are two ways to bring a civil claim into federal court. You can bring a diversity claim or you can bring a claim involving a federal question.

A diversity claim is one wherein the parties are of diverse citizenship. A citizen of the state of Connecticut may sue a citizen of the state of Massachusetts in the federal court in Massachusetts. That difference or diversity of citizenship establishes one of the elements of a diversity claim. The diversity claim, however, must also involve a claim involving a monetary controversy where the amount at stake is in excess of $75,000.00 over and above any interest that may be claimed and over and above any attorneys fees that may be claimed. The civil jurisdiction of the federal courts is legislated by Congress. Congress has chosen to limit the overall civil jurisdiction of the federal courts. The logic behind that is that civil litigants can always go into state court to resolve their civil disputes and as such the federal courts should be reserved only for certain types of disputes. Disputes between citizens of different states may be subject to some local or regional prejudice if brought in state court and therefore Congress has decided that these types of civil claims, provided they meet the monetary amount set forth above, can be brought in federal court in order to avoid the potential prejudice or bias that a citizen of one state might meet by suing a citizen of another state in that citizen's state court system.

The second way of bringing a civil claim into federal court is by suing under a federal statute or a federal constitutional provision. For instance, if I file a civil rights claim against my employer, even though I may be a citizen of Virginia and my employer may be a citizen of Virginia, I can still bring that claim in federal court because the claim is brought under federal law. Likewise, if I pursue a claim against a defendant under some theory involving a violation of my constitutional rights, then that type of claim may be brought in federal court because it is founded upon a federal constitutional issue. Federal question cases do not have any monetary jurisdictional limits as do diversity claims. That is, the discrimination claim that I bring against my employer may only be worth one hundred dollars but I can still bring that claim in federal court.

Another element of jurisdiction that is somewhat different is the question of personal jurisdiction. This has been previously discussed in the section above dealing with the state court civil system. In order to file suit against a person in the state of Massachusetts, either in state or federal court, I have to assert and be able to prove that the court (state or federal) has personal jurisdiction over that defendant. Personal jurisdiction can be obtained in a number of different ways. For instance if the defendant committed the alleged wrong in the state of Massachusetts then that would give the courts (state or federal) within that state personal jurisdiction over him. If the defendant lives in the state of Massachusetts, then the courts (state or federal) in that state would have personal jurisdiction over him. If the defendant has engaged in a course of conduct wherein he has substantial contacts with the state of Massachusetts and the claim in question arose out of those contacts then that may likewise give the courts (state and federal) personal jurisdiction over him in the state of Massachusetts. The concept of personal jurisdiction is entirely separate and distinct from the concept of the subject matter jurisdiction. We talked about the subject matter jurisdiction of the federal courts in terms of civil claims having to be founded upon diversity or a federal question. That relates exclusively to what is called subject matter jurisdiction. Personal jurisdiction deals with the issue of whether the court has authority over that defendant to litigate that claim. The concept of personal jurisdiction is founded on the idea that it would be unfair to cause a citizen of California to have to litigate a claim in Massachusetts unless that citizen of California had done something that would constitute some substantial contact with the state of Massachusetts which gave rise to the claim in question. As such, the mere fact that a federal court may have subject matter jurisdiction to litigate your claim does not necessarily mean that it has personal jurisdiction over the defendant to litigate that claim.

Lawyers frequently argue over the respective merits of bringing a civil claim in state court versus federal court. Some members of the legal profession maintain that it is always to the advantage of the plaintiff to litigate a claim in federal court because the Federal Rules of Evidence typically are a bit more lenient and therefore more favorable to a plaintiff than are the state rules of evidence; the federal courtrooms are much grander and larger than are the typical state courtrooms and therefore juries are likely to be more impressed with a case brought in federal court and therefore more likely to return a verdict more favorable to the plaintiff; and also because federal judges are sometimes considered to be of a higher caliber than are state court judges. Those types of reasons obviously are very subjective and there are probably as many lawyers across the nation who feel that it is more in the interest of a plaintiff to file suit in state court than it is in federal court. In any event, since it is the plaintiff who initiates a lawsuit, the plaintiff has the opportunity to some extent to choose the forum. Even though a suit may be initiated in state court, if in fact the subject matter jurisdiction requirements as set forth above have been met, then the defendant may remove that case from state court to federal court.

Once a case has been initiated in federal court, the process that is followed is much the same as what has been described previously in the state court system. The particular procedural rules that are followed in federal court may differ to some extent from what are followed in state court but the basic procedure is much the same once the lawsuit has been initiated.

A federal court when hearing a diversity case is in essence sitting as if it were a state court. The federal judge who is being called upon to make rulings of law has to apply the pertinent state law that governs that transaction. If a citizen of Connecticut sues a citizen from Massachusetts in a federal court in Massachusetts for an automobile accident that occurred in the state of Connecticut, then the federal judge in Massachusetts is going to apply Connecticut law to that claim. Massachusetts law on the particular issues in questions may be markedly different than Connecticut law.

A federal judge, however, who is hearing a federal question case typically is going to apply federal law since the claim itself arose under federal law.

A federal judge even though he may be called upon to apply state law in a diversity claim is still bound by the Federal Rules of Procedure which govern the civil procedure in that court system and is also bound by the Federal Rules of Evidence which are the rules that govern the admissibility of evidence in the federal court system. As such, a federal judge when sitting in a diversity claim is called upon to apply a number of different types of law; i.e., both state law and federal law to different aspects of the case.

C. <u>CRIMINAL JUSTICE IN THE STATE COURT SYSTEM</u>

Within the criminal justice system, there are several players: the police, the prosecutors, the judges, the parole and probation officers and then of course the accused who is also called the defendant. Criminal prosecutions are typically initiated by the police by making an arrest. That arrest may be made as a result of a crime witnessed by a police officer or may be made as a result of an investigation by the police. Once the police have made that arrest, then the person arrested will begin to wind his way through the criminal justice system.

In terms of describing that journey through the criminal justice system, the best place to begin of course is at the beginning. We have previously discussed various aspects of constitutional law. Our most frequent encounter with constitutional law is found within the criminal context. Criminal law and procedure to a great extent is constitutional law.

You may recall that the Bill of Rights (the first ten amendments to the Constitution) initially were only restrictions on the power of the federal government. The criminal process, however, is exercised not only by the federal government but also by the state government. During the early years of our government, the Bill of Rights in large measure were not considered to have any application to criminal prosecutions in state court. Over the last fifty years, there has been a process of "selective incorporation" wherein the rights guaranteed to defendants in criminal prosecutions have been selectively incorporated into state prosecutions so that at this point in time virtually all of the rights set forth in the Bill of Rights apply not only to federal criminal prosecutions but also to state criminal prosecutions. As such, a defendants' right to remain silent, the right to competent counsel, the right to confront his accusers, the right to be free from cruel and unusual punishment, and most of the other rights set forth in the Fourth, Fifth, Sixth and Eighth Amendments to the Constitution have been made applicable to defendants charged with crimes in the state court system.

Many of the rights that we associate with a criminal prosecution are rights that come into play before an arrest is ever made. The Fourth Amendment says that we have a right to be free of unreasonable police searches and seizures. That means that the police cannot stop you while you are walking down the street unless they have some reasonable justification for believing that you either have committed a criminal offense or are about to commit a criminal offense. If a police officer sees you walking down the street engaging in some unusual behavior, stops you to question you about this and sees a conspicuous bulge under your coat that looks like it may be a pistol, then he may stop you and pat you down to determine whether that conspicuous bulge is in fact a pistol. If in fact it is a pistol and you are not allowed to be carrying such a concealed weapon then you may be arrested. If a police officer receives a report that a bank has just been robbed and there is a description of the perpetrators broadcast over the police radio and that police officer feels that you fit that description as he sees you walking down the street, then he may stop you and question you as to where you have been, where you are going and request your identity. If he is not satisfied at that point that you are not the suspect, then he may even take you back to the scene of the offense to see if you can be identified by any of the witnesses to the crime. If you are then identified by one of the witnesses to the crime, you will be arrested. A police officer, however, may not stop you and detain you while you walk down the street simply on his whim that you look suspicious or unsavory. Instead he must have some reason that can be articulated that would cause a reasonable person to conclude that you have committed some criminal offense or are about to commit a criminal offense.

You probably have heard the saying that "a man's home is his castle". Indeed, that is true insofar as police searches are concerned. The police cannot randomly come into your home and conduct a search. Generally the police need to have a search warrant to conduct a search of a premises but in certain emergency circumstances they may be allowed to come into the premises and conduct a search if that is necessary in order to accomplish an arrest of a person who they believe has committed a crime or if it is necessary to prevent the destruction of evidence. If time permits, however, the police are required to obtain a warrant issued by a judge or magistrate authorizing the search and entry into your home or premises.

A rule that has evolved over the years that is the subject of a good deal of controversy is the so called "exclusionary rule". What that rule says is that if the police violate a defendant's constitutional rights and as a result of that violation acquire evidence that otherwise could be used against that defendant then the courts will exclude that evidence if it was obtained as the result of an unreasonable search or seizure. That statement of the exclusionary rule is a rather general one and over the years the courts have applied several exceptions to the exclusionary rule. The intent of the exclusionary rule is to control police behavior. It is felt that if the police recognize that evidence that they obtain in violation of someone's constitutional rights cannot be used in a criminal prosecution, then the police will control their own behavior so as to assure that the constitutional rights of defendants are in fact observed. The battle over the exclusionary rule has raged for nearly forty years with some people arguing that it makes no sense to allow the criminal to go free simply because the constable has bungled. People on the other side of the issue, however, argue that the only way that the constable can be controlled is by excluding evidence that he obtains illegally.

In order for a defendant to assert the exclusionary rule, he must assert and prove that he has standing to challenge the alleged constitutional violation. This requirement of standing, or having an appropriate interest in the outcome of the case, is a general requirement for asserting any constitutional right. An example of where a defendant would not have standing arises where an illegal arrest of defendant A leads to the seizure of narcotics in the home of defendant B and the subsequent arrest of defendant C at another location. The narcotics in that case could not be used in evidence against A because A has standing to object to the illegal arrest but could be introduced against C because C has no standing to object because it was not his home that was illegally searched and he was not the one who was illegally arrested. As such in that case C would not have standing to raise that constitutional violation in order to exclude the evidence.

Once a person has been arrested, then the arresting officer is allowed to search that person and also to search the area within arm's reach of that person. Anything that is found as a result of that type of search incident to the arrest may be used against the defendant. Likewise, if there is some illegal substance or item that is within plain view of the officer while he makes the arrest then that likewise may be seized and used against that defendant. Vehicle searches are frequently the subject of controversy. When a motor vehicle operator is arrested and taken to the police station typically his vehicle is impounded. Are the police then authorized to search the vehicle? As a general rule they are mainly for purposes of conducting an inventory search of the vehicle. That is, since the vehicle has come into their possession, it is in the interest of the police to determine whether there are any items of value within that vehicle so that they are not later charged with a misappropriation of those items. They typically will conduct an inventory search of the vehicle and if there is some illegal substance or material found in the vehicle then that likewise could be the basis of a criminal prosecution.

The general criteria for making an arrest is what is referred to as probable cause. Probable cause arises where there is sufficient evidence to cause a reasonable person to believe that the defendant probably committed the crime in question. The key word there is <u>probable</u>. Indeed in the Legal Dictionary I believe the two most important words are "probable" and "certainty." Let me start with the second word first. There are a precious few things in life that we can say we are certain of. We may be certain of our own name and where we live but aside from that there are not too many things in life that we are absolutely certain of. As such, it would be a bit unrealistic for the law to expect certainty in terms of proof. What is typically expected is probability. That is, that something is more likely than not likely or more probable than not probable. That is the typical standard in civil litigation when it comes to proving something. In a criminal case the standard of proof for purposes of proving whether someone is guilty is guilt beyond a reasonable doubt. Guilt beyond a reasonable doubt is not equivalent to absolute certainty. Something, however, is probable if it is more likely than not likely. If something is more likely than not likely or if the scales have been tipped by so much as a featherweight in favor of the question at issue, then it is deemed to be probable.

The police may rely upon a variety of different sources of information to arrive at what is referred to as probable cause. For instance, a police investigator who is relying upon an informant that he has used in the past about drug activities may determine that there is probable cause that narcotics are being sold at a particular location and that may justify not only the issuance of a search warrant for those premises but the arrest of the persons inside the premises if in fact narcotics are found. Probable cause may also be founded upon police surveillance wherein the police have actually seen suspicious activities going on at a particular location that seems to follow the pattern of drug activity and in addition may have reports from neighbors of suspicious activities at that same location that are in the nature of drug activities and all of that may then justify the issuance of a warrant and a search of the premises.

In the criminal field, there are two different types of warrants that may be issued: arrest warrants and search warrants. An arrest warrant is an authorization or an order issued by a judge or magistrate authorizing the arrest of a particular person for a particular crime. A search warrant is an order or an authorization issued by a judge or magistrate authorizing the police to conduct a search of a specific premises looking for specific objects. Although the police do not always have to have a search warrant before conducting a search of a premises, generally it is preferred that they do especially if time permits. In some circumstances, however, time does not permit the police to go to the local courthouse, find a judge who has time to review the situation with them and obtain a search warrant. In those types of emergency circumstances wherein evidence is about to be destroyed or wherein the crime is in progress, then the police may enter the premises of another and conduct a search without a warrant.

If a search warrant has been issued, then the warrant may actually indicate when the search is to be conducted. Typically the matter of when the search warrant is to be served and executed is a matter of discretion for the police. Once the police have arrived at the premises they are expected to announce their entry although if they have some reasonable cause to fear that evidence is being destroyed or that the police themselves may be in danger as a result of the criminal suspects being aware of their presence, then the police may not have to announce their presence but may enter without notice. Once the police have entered the premises, then anyone in the premises is going to be detained pending the completion of that search. If in fact illegal materials or the items that are sought are found on the premises and if there is probable cause to believe that the persons on the premises have something to do with the commission of the crime at issue then they may be arrested and charged with a criminal violation.

Sometimes the police may request a citizen to consent to a search either of their person or of their premises. Nobody has to give such consent. If a person does consent to the search of their physical person or their home then that is considered to be a consensual search and obviously in that type of circumstance the police do not need a warrant.

Police sometimes are called upon to engage in various types of surveillance techniques consisting of wire tapping and electronic eavesdropping. That type of surveillance is controlled either by specific state or federal statutes and as a general rule a warrant is necessary before the police can engage in that type of activity.

One of the most notable decisions of the Supreme Court over the last forty years involving criminal procedure is the Miranda decision. The Miranda case involved the Fifth Amendment to the U.S. Constitution and related specifically to the rights of a criminal suspect after he had been detained by the police. The Miranda case held that the Fifth Amendment right against self incrimination meant that a person upon being arrested, before he could be questioned by the police, had a right to be advised of his right to remain silent, his right to counsel and his right to terminate any police interrogation once it has begun. Miranda does not require that these rights be given to every person who is arrested. Frequently a person is arrested and the police have no intention of asking him any questions about the alleged criminal activity. If, however, the police do begin asking questions about the alleged criminal activity, then they are required to give the Miranda rights. If those rights are not given and the defendant divulges information in response to police questioning, then that evidence may be excluded at trial. If the defendant spontaneously volunteers information, then in that type of circumstance there is no Miranda requirement and therefore the evidence would not be excluded. The scope of Miranda has been expanded by different courts and generally is held now to apply not only to persons who have been arrested but also to persons who have become a focus of a police investigation. That is, even though a particular suspect has not been arrested if in fact he has become the focus of that criminal investigation and the interrogation is what is deemed to be custodial; i.e., taking place in a police station or another type of police environment, then in that context the police must give the <u>Miranda</u> rights to that suspect before conducting their interrogation. A suspect or a defendant of course can waive that right against self incrimination and is free to speak to the police about his involvement in criminal activities. Experienced police officers normally require that that waiver be in writing or be recorded so that there is no question that the suspect or defendant is in fact voluntarily and knowingly waiving his rights.

Once a defendant has been charged and arrested by the police then his case is reviewed either by a prosecuting attorney or a magistrate. Magistrates are judicial officers who fulfill some of the functions of a judge but do not have the complete authority of a judge. The purpose of having the case reviewed by the prosecuting attorney or the magistrate at the early stages of the process is to determine whether the police in fact did have probable cause to believe that the defendant had committed the crime in question. If the magistrate or prosecuting attorney makes that determination, then normally the case will move on to the next stage. Also at the early stages of the process, the court will set bail. Bail is typically set by a magistrate or a judge who considers the seriousness of the offense, the likelihood of the defendant fleeing the jurisdiction and then establishes a monetary amount that must be paid to secure the defendant's appearance at all subsequent court procedures. That bail can be paid in a cash amount or may be paid in the form of security against a piece of real estate or more often is paid by the posting of a bond written by a bail bondsman. A bond issued by a bail bondsman is a type of insurance policy wherein the court is the beneficiary of that policy. The defendant who obtains the bond from the bail bondsman pays a premium for that bond which normally is a certain percentage of the face amount of the bond and in turn if the defendant does not appear at subsequent court proceedings then the bondsman has to pay that bond amount to the court. The bondsman then will frequently use a bounty hunter to go out and find that defendant and return him to the court so that the bondsman can redeem his bond; i.e., get his money back that he had to pay to the court pursuant to the bond. The Eighth Amendment provides that "excessive bail shall not be required". That is a rather loose standard and indeed the amount of bail that will be set by the court is a very subjective matter.

Early in the course of a criminal proceeding, the defendant will be brought into court and the charges brought against him by the government will be formally read to him and he will be asked by the court whether he pleads guilty or not guilty to the charge. At that stage of the proceeding the defendant is expected to have an attorney unless he has waived his right to have an attorney. If the defendant cannot afford to have an attorney and meets the local guidelines for the appointment of counsel then the court will appoint an attorney to represent him in that criminal case.

At any point during this process the defendant may plead guilty to the charge leveled against him. Likewise, at any stage during the process, the defendant or his attorney may conduct negotiations with the prosecutor to determine whether a plea to some lesser charge may be agreeable to the government. If such an agreement is reached then the plea agreement is brought to the attention of the court and the prosecution is at that point concluded with the only thing left to be done is the imposition of whatever sentence has either been agreed to or is otherwise established by the court.

In most criminal prosecutions, the defendant has the right to appear at a preliminary hearing wherein some or all of the prosecution witnesses will be called for the purpose of presenting evidence to determine whether there is probable cause to support the arrest made by the police. This hearing is normally presided over by a judge or magistrate. The sole issue for determination at this preliminary hearing is simply whether probable cause exists. If in fact probable cause is found to exist, then the next stage in the proceeding is presentation of the case to a grand jury. A grand jury is a group of citizens who are convened by the court for the purpose of reviewing criminal cases as presented to them by the prosecutor to determine again whether there is probable cause to believe that the defendant committed the crime that he is charged with. The grand jury can choose to indict the defendant for that criminal offense or can choose not to indict. Grand juries are frequently referred to as being rubber stamps of the prosecutor's office. The grand jury, although it is composed of unbiased citizens, only hears one side of the story. The only evidence that is presented at a grand jury is evidence that is chosen by the prosecutor which normally comes in through the testimony of police officers. As such the grand jurors are not hearing from the defendant and are not hearing the other side of the story. As one might expect, grand juries typically accept the recommendation of the prosecutor and go ahead and indict the defendant for the crime that he is charged with.

Criminal offenses can be divided into two general categories: felonies and misdemeanors. A felony is a crime for which a person can be imprisoned for more than a year. A misdemeanor is an offense for which a person can be imprisoned for up to a year. The criminal process in regards to misdemeanors may differ dramatically from the criminal process as it applies to felonies. The defendant charged with a felony is entitled to greater protections and as such the procedure in regards to a felony case may be considerably more prolonged than that involving a misdemeanor. It is not at all unusual that in regards to a misdemeanor charge, the defendant simply appears in court on one occasion and after being advised of his right to have an attorney the case is tried on that one occasion. A felony charge may result, however, in several court appearances: first with a hearing in regards to the setting of bond, then an arraignment, then a preliminary hearing, then an appearance for the setting of a trial date, then the appearance for any pre-trial motions and then finally the appearance for trial.

In some criminal prosecutions pre-trial discovery may be allowed. The discovery that is allowed in a criminal case is considerably more limited than what is allowed in a civil case. In a civil case, the prevailing philosophy is that a full disclosure of the facts and full discovery of the strong points and weak points of the other party's case is desirable in order to allow the parties to make an intelligent decision as to whether the case should be settled and, if so, how much it should be settled for. In the area of criminal law, the prevailing philosophy is that too much discovery is not a good thing because the information gathered by the defendant could conceivably be used to intimidate witnesses and to otherwise bog down the criminal justice system. As such, the amount of discovery allowed in a criminal case is fairly limited compared to what is allowed in a civil case.

Under the Sixth Amendment to the Constitution, a defendant in a criminal case has the right to a jury trial. That right to a jury trial is not unlimited in that it may not apply to what are referred to as petty offenses. An offense may be characterized as petty if it carries a penalty of potential imprisonment of less than six months. Many states have expanded that right and grant jury trials for any offense that carries potential imprisonment. The right to a jury trial in some states applies to both sides; i.e., not only does the defendant have the right to request a jury trial but also the government has the right to request a jury trial.

The jury in a criminal case in most jurisdictions consists of twelve people. In most jurisdictions the jury verdict must be unanimous.

The stages of a jury trial in a criminal case are much the same as those previously described in a civil case. Each side has the right to conduct voir dire of the jury in order to determine whether there are any members of the potential jury that may have any bias or predisposition about the case. Once a jury has been selected, then the prosecution has the right to make an opening statement followed by the defendant's opening statement and then the government's presentation of evidence. At the conclusion of the government's case, the defendant has a right to make a motion to dismiss the government's case on the grounds of it being insufficient to justify conviction. Typically that motion is denied by the court and then the defendant has the right to present his evidence. A distinguishing characteristic of a criminal trial is that the government may not call the defendant to the witness stand. That is the defendant has an absolute right to be free of self incrimination. Only the defendant can make the decision as to whether he testifies. Once the defendant chooses to testify, then he is subject to cross examination by the prosecutor.

Some criminal cases attract a good deal of press coverage. If the press coverage has been so intensive that the local pool of potential jurors has been influenced, then it is conceivable that the case could be moved from that jurisdiction to another locale where the press coverage has not been as intense. The press cannot be excluded from a criminal proceeding involving an adult. The Sixth Amendment to the Constitution guarantees the accused the right to a public trial and likewise, the First Amendment guarantees the right of the public and the press to attend criminal trials. Most courts in the U.S. do restrict the use of cameras in the courtroom. This is generally considered to be a means of controlling conduct in the courtroom and is not necessarily intended to restrict the right of the press to be present.

A trial, whether a civil case or a criminal case, is designed to be a truth seeking activity. The truth seeking capability of a trial on the civil side is frequently somewhat affected by the disparity in ability between lawyers. That likewise can apply in regards to a criminal case although there are some aspects of a criminal case that are designed to level the playing field between the government and the defense. A prosecutor who is aware of information that is considered to be exculpatory; i.e., that would tend to show that the defendant is not guilty, must disclose that information to the defense prior to trial. The rationale behind that rule is based upon the truth seeking function of a trial. A criminal trial is not simply a matter of gamesmanship, but is a matter of getting all of the pertinent facts out before the jury and then letting the jury decide whether the defendant is guilty or not guilty. During the course of the trial a prosecutor is somewhat restricted as to the vehemence of his arguments to the jury. That is, a prosecutor is subject to the general due process prohibition against prejudicial and inflammatory remarks to the jury.

A defendant in any criminal case has the right to confront his accusers. This right of confrontation means that the defendant has an absolute right to be present at trial. Of course if the defendant engages in outrageous behavior, then he can be restrained or placed in a separate room where he can see and hear the proceedings but not disrupt the proceedings. That, however, is a rather extraordinary measure in a criminal case. That right of confrontation also means that the defense has a rather broad right as far as cross examining those witnesses who testify against the defendant. In addition, that right of confrontation restricts the right of the government to put in evidence statements of persons who do not testify at trial. Such statements generally would be classified as hearsay and therefore not admissible. In a criminal case those hearsay statements further become objectionable because they may violate the defendant's right to confront his accusers.

The standard of proof in a criminal case is what is referred to as proof beyond a reasonable doubt. We have previously discussed the standards that may apply in civil cases as being a preponderance of the evidence (more than 50%) and clear and convincing evidence in cases such as fraud claims. Proof beyond a reasonable doubt is a standard higher than either of those. Proof beyond a reasonable doubt does not mean that the jury has to be absolutely certain of the defendant's guilt but if a juror has a "reasonable doubt" as to whether the defendant is guilty then that juror should vote not guilty Since a unanimous verdict is required in most jurisdictions in a criminal case, one juror who believes he has a reasonable doubt can hang up a jury and prevent the government from getting a conviction. If the jury deliberations result in an eleven (11) to one (1) vote in favor of conviction; i.e., guilty, then typically the trial court will, on motion of the government, declare a mistrial and thereby allow the government to re-try the case.

The final stage of a criminal case in the trial court is that of sentencing. The federal judiciary as well as many states now operates under sentencing guidelines. These sentencing guidelines are very detailed and very complex guidelines or formulas that govern the parameters of a sentence that a judge can impose on a defendant for a specific crime. Within those sentencing guidelines there are a variety of factors that may be considered by the court including but not limited to the defendant's prior history, the defendant's cooperation with the government in the investigation of other related crimes, the defendant's feelings of remorse after conviction and of course the nature and seriousness of the offense itself. The purpose of these sentencing guidelines is to eliminate the significant disparity that can exist from one judge to another in terms of sentences for the same crime. The judiciary, to some extent, has been rather critical of sentencing guidelines because they do significantly restrict a judge's discretion. The guidelines, however, do allow for exceptional circumstances wherein the guidelines may not be strictly applied.

After a sentence has been imposed the defendant has the right to pursue an appeal. All states now provide for appellate review. The availability of that appellate review cannot be conditioned upon the convicted defendant's financial status. If a trial transcript of the proceedings is required in order to pursue an appeal, then the government must provide that transcript for the indigent defendant. Likewise, the state must provide counsel for an appeal to an indigent defendant. Once a defendant has been found not guilty the government has no right to appeal that finding. The logic of this rule is that to allow appeals by the government would essentially allow the government to potentially utilize its vast resources to essentially wear down the defendant.

The double jeopardy clause of the Fifth Amendment provides that no person shall be tried twice for the same offense. Jeopardy is deemed to attach in jury trials once the jury is impaneled and sworn. The double jeopardy prohibition, however, is somewhat flexible. That is, if a mistrial is declared before a verdict is reached due to the inability of a jury to reach a unanimous verdict or for some other reason other than misconduct on the part of the prosecution, then that would not be deemed to be a violation of the double jeopardy clause. Double jeopardy also only applies to the sovereign who is bringing the charge. For instance, if you rob a bank you could be charged with a violation of that under state law. You could also then be prosecuted for that same bank robbery under federal law. That dual prosecution would not be a violation of the double jeopardy clause.

After sentencing and after all appeals have been exhausted, a criminal defendant may pursue another avenue in order to have his case reviewed. That avenue is what is referred to as a habeas corpus petition. The term habeas corpus literally means "you have the body". A habeas corpus petition is a petition to a court requesting that the court compel the government to justify or explain what may appear to be some irregularity in the prosecution of that defendant. That is, a defendant who has been tried in state court and found guilty may appeal that conviction up through the state court system, through the intermediate court of appeals if one exists in that state, and then to the high court of that state. After having exhausted those appeals he may file a petition for habeas corpus in federal court requesting that the federal judge direct the state authorities to show cause why this defendant should not be released from incarceration because of what may be deemed to be some irregularity in that state court prosecution. Although habeas corpus petitions were much more common years ago, the courts more recently have somewhat restricted the rights of defendants to pursue that type of relief.

D. **CRIMINAL JUSTICE IN THE FEDERAL COURT SYSTEM**

The procedure by which a criminal case is handled in the federal court is not dramatically different than that described above for the state courts. Within the federal court system, there are a specific set of rules called the Federal Rules of Criminal Procedure that govern the conduct of a criminal case. Within the federal system, the law enforcement agency initiating the prosecution rather than being a local police department is a federal law enforcement agency such as the F.B.I., Secret Service or other such federal agency. Cases in federal court will be prosecuted by the U.S. Attorney's office that operates within that federal district. Crimes that are committed within that federal district will be tried within the U.S. District Court that has jurisdiction for that federal district and will be subject then to appeal to the Circuit Court of Appeals that covers that federal district.

One of the distinguishing features of the federal courts is that they are courts of limited jurisdiction. The Chief Justice of the U.S. Supreme Court has recently requested that Congress stop expanding the criminal jurisdiction of the federal courts. Congress over the last several years has enacted federal criminal statutes dealing with such things as carjacking and non-payment of child support. Those traditionally have been offenses that would have been governed exclusively by state law and prosecuted exclusively in state court. The Congress having passed federal legislation dealing with those issues now they may be prosecuted also in federal court. That expanding criminal jurisdiction of the federal courts has been slow moving but fairly steady over the last several years. Our founding fathers would probably say that this ever expanding scope of federal legislation is contrary to their intent. Indeed, it probably is contrary to their intent and as such may be subject to constitutional challenge.

E. <u>JUVENILE COURT</u>

Juvenile Court is sometimes referred to by lawyers and law enforcement officers as "Kiddie Court". The Juvenile Court in some jurisdictions, however, can be more than simply what the name may imply. It may in some jurisdictions actually be a type of Family Court wherein all different types of family disputes may also be resolved. I am not going to deal in this section with family law issues but rather simply deal with issues of juvenile justice.

The logic behind the Juvenile Court system in the United States is that because juveniles are underage they should be dealt with in a different fashion than adults. In many jurisdictions juvenile offenses are not even referred to as criminal offenses. Juvenile records in most jurisdictions are strictly confidential and are not subject to public access either by means of subpoena or other inquiry. As such, a person who as a juvenile is arrested and processed through the Juvenile Court does not have to report that offense on a job application or other type of inquiry unless expressly asked about it since the inquiry itself is not going to be subject to any public confirmation.

Proceedings in Juvenile court are all conducted by a judge with no jury present. For certain types of offenses, however, a juvenile may be transferred to the adult system and may be tried as an adult with all the consequences that might apply to an adult. That type of treatment is generally reserved for the more serious offenses.

An offense in Juvenile Court is generally handled in a somewhat informal fashion. There may be a prosecutor present in Juvenile Court. That prosecutor represents the interest of the government or the victim. The prosecutor may present evidence in front of the judge who then hears also from the defense and then renders a decision. That decision normally consists of a finding of whether the Juvenile is "involved" and if so there may be some punishment imposed. That punishment may consist simply of a monetary fine, may consist of performing some community service or for more extreme circumstances may involve confinement to a Juvenile Home for a period of time.

The significant thing to keep in mind in regards to Juvenile Courts is that they are " a breed apart." The thrust of the Juvenile Court system is to be instructive and rehabilitative; i.e, to instruct the juvenile as to the error of his ways and to assist him with rehabilitation. That is dramatically different from the thrust of the Adult Court system which although may have an element of rehabilitation about it, is more oriented toward simply a finding of guilt or innocence and then punishing the guilty.

F. **TRAFFIC COURT**

The Traffic Court in most jurisdictions is a branch of the criminal division of that court. Traffic offenses although not normally thought of as being criminal offenses really are criminal offenses because they do involve a potential criminal penalty. That criminal penalty may consist simply of a monetary fine although for more serious traffic offenses there may be actual arrest and imprisonment.

In most jurisdictions traffic offenses are handled in a very perfunctory fashion with a single judge hearing perhaps hundreds of cases in the course of a few hours. In most instances, these cases are presented by a police officer who simply stands before the judge and tells the judge what the officer saw. If there are witnesses involved then those witnesses may be called who will be given an opportunity to briefly explain what happened. The defendant then is given an opportunity to explain what happened if he wishes. The defendant, however, has no obligation to testify since his Fifth Amendment right against self incrimination would apply in this proceeding.

If you have ever been to Traffic Court, you probably recall seeing a multitude of police officers in the court room. Those police officers are there to testify in regards to cases wherein they have issued tickets or made arrests. If, for some reason, the officer issuing the ticket does not show up for the Traffic Court date then typically the case will be dismissed for lack of prosecution by the government. Likewise, if there was a witness to the traffic offense and the witness is the only one who can establish the government's case, if that witness does not show up for the traffic hearing then the case may be dismissed for that reason. You may recall that we had talked previously that the burden rests with the government to prove it's case in a criminal prosecution. That burden applies in a traffic case. The Government cannot prove it's case simply through your testimony but rather must present independent evidence either from a Police Officer or a witness to establish what happened. If the Government cannot do that then the Government cannot meet it's burden of proof and therefore the charge against you will be dismissed without you ever having testified.

In some jurisdictions, Traffic Court cases are handled administratively and they are actually presided over by an administrative hearing officer. An Administrative Hearing Officer is a type of quasi-judge who has all of the authority of a judge although does not necessarily have that title and may not wear a robe in the hearing room.

G. **WHAT TO EXPECT IF CALLED AS A JUROR**

As citizens, we all have an obligation to serve as jurors when summoned. Your summons to appear as a juror may come from a State Court or from a Federal Court. Jurors are chosen by different means in different jurisdictions. Some jurisdictions draw from records of the Department of Motor Vehicles, property owner records and voting records. Other jurisdictions may draw from only one or two of the above. Lawyers and Judges have debated the merits of how jurors should be chosen for many years. Most judges are probably of the feeling that jurors should be drawn from voting lists and also from property ownership roles because that tends to produce a group of citizens that are more involved in the community. People, however, that are simply listed with the Department of Motor Vehicles as being licensed drivers but who are not voters or property owners may be less involved in their community. The merits of the respective positions on that issue lies in the eyes of the beholder.

In any event, if you are called as a juror you must respond unless you are subject to one of the exemptions that apply in that jurisdiction. Over the last several years the number of exemptions that have applied has been narrowed in most states. It used to be that the exemptions were so broad that the court frequently was left with the only eligible jurors being housewives. That is not in anyway to diminish the ability of housewives to decide the merits of litigation, but the purpose of our jury system is to provide a broad cross section of the population and not to limit it to one occupational group or to any one group at all.

When you are called as a juror, you will have the opportunity to state any particular problems you may have with serving. In most instances, however, unless the reason why you cannot serve is extremely compelling and virtually of an emergency nature then your excuse for not serving will be rejected by the Court. Your initial selection for service in a courtroom is a matter of a random draw. A certain number of jurors will be sent to a particular courtroom assigned to a judge who has been assigned a particular case. Once you are sent to that courtroom, the judge may ask you certain preliminary questions that are designed to determine whether there is something that would automatically disqualify you. Then the lawyers (or in some cases the judge himself) will have the opportunity to conduct what is called Voir Dire which is a process by which you may be questioned to determine whether you have any particular bias or interest in the outcome of the case. If you do then you may be challenged for that reason.

If a case is going to last for several days there may alternate jurors chosen. Typically those alternate jurors will not be identified to the jury members themselves since if you were to know that you were an alternate that may affect the level of attention that you apply to the case. Once all of the evidence is concluded and the closing arguments have been completed then the alternate juror typically will be excused.

One thing that frequently comes up during the course of jury service is whether or not jurors are allowed to take notes and/or to ask questions during the course of the proceeding. That is a matter of discretion of the individual judge and can vary dramatically from state to state and from courtroom to courtroom. Some judges allow jurors to take notes, others do not. Some judges allow jurors to ask questions while others do not.

The logic behind the jury system is that since the parties themselves are not able to resolve the particular dispute that has been brought to the courtroom, the best way of resolving that dispute is to have a group of unbiased citizens hear the evidence in an objective fashion and then decide that case fairly based solely upon the evidence presented to them in the courtroom. Trial lawyers will tell you that the jury system is the great equalizer. The lowliest citizen in this country can sue the mightiest corporation and when those two parties come before a jury they are equal. The jury is to treat each party with the same respect and attention. The proponents of tort reform maintain that the jury system is a system that has gone awry. They maintain that jurors frequently award outlandish sums for ridiculous cases. Although it is not unheard of that juries do sometimes "runaway" that is very much the exception. Even if the jury does do something that is contrary to the evidence and the law as given to them, the trial judge always has the authority to correct that by reversing the jury verdict or in a civil case by reducing the amount of the verdict if it is too high.

H. **WHAT TO EXPECT IF CALLED AS A WITNESS**

Any party to a lawsuit or a criminal proceeding has the authority to subpoena witnesses. That power to subpoena witnesses is a basic constitutional right since witnesses are the primary form by which evidence is presented. If a party cannot present witnesses then obviously it cannot present its evidence in support of its case. The way a witness is compelled to appear in court is by means of a subpoena. The word subpoena literally means "under penalty". A subpoena very simply is a court order directing a person to appear at a particular place and time for the purposes of giving testimony. That subpoena may be for you to appear at a trial or to appear at a deposition. A deposition is a means of discovery conducted in most civil litigation wherein the attorneys have the opportunity to question witnesses as to what they know about a particular event relevant to that lawsuit.

If you should be served with a subpoena the subpoena will typically indicate the name and address and phone number of the attorney that requested you to appear. You should feel free to call that attorney and find out why you have been subpoenaed. If the date and time of the subpoena is not convenient for you then you should inquire as to whether that date and time can be changed. If the attorney tells you that the date and time cannot be changed and you simply are not able to appear then you need to bring that to the attention of the court immediately so that issue can be resolved by the court.

If you are subpoenaed to appear for trial or for a deposition then the local rules of the court may also require that attorney to pay you a fee for your traveling expenses and/or a fee for time that you lose from work. That is something that is governed by state law and is something that you should inquire into.

Sometimes witnesses ask whether they themselves can ask question during the course of the proceeding. Typically the answer to that question is "no". You have been subpoenaed to give information and not to make inquiries on your own. That does not mean that during the course of a proceeding you may not stop and ask the judge a question. If a bonafide question occurs to you, you should ask it. The judge may tell you that he cannot answer that question or in some instances may provide you with an appropriate answer. The purpose of your appearing to testify is to respond to particular questions that are asked of you by the attorneys, the parties or the court. Once that questioning by all of the attorneys involved has been completed then you will be excused and allowed to proceed about your normal business. In some instances after you have finished testifying the judge may tell you that you have to remain in the courthouse because you may be called again as a witness. If that presents a problem for you as far as your own scheduling then you need to bring that to the attention of the court immediately so that the issue can be dealt with. Most judges and attorneys are willing to work with witnesses in order to accommodate their schedule. The burden, however, is upon the witness to bring those issues to the attention of the court or the attorney.

III. AREAS OF THE LAW THAT MOST OFTEN IMPACT YOUR LIFE

A. CONTRACTS

A contract is an agreement between two persons to either do something or not to do something in exchange for some form of consideration.

Let us take a look at each of those terms within that definition. An agreement may come in several different forms. The agreement may be implied as a result of the conduct of the parties. On the other hand, the agreement may be expressed, meaning that the parties have expressly stated what their intentions are and what they wish to obtain as a result of the agreement. An expressed contract may be in writing or it may be oral. Either type of contract is equally enforceable in most instances although obviously a written contract is always preferable because it expressly sets forth the terms of the agreement in black and white. An oral contract is always subject to dispute because the parties may have different recollections of exactly what they agreed to.

The way that an agreement comes about is generally through an offer being made by one party and then that offer being accepted by the other party. For instance, if I were to send you a letter offering to paint your house for one hundred dollars with such work to be accomplished by a certain date and you then wrote on the bottom of the letter that these terms were agreeable and sent that back to me then that letter would constitute a written contract. The offer was in the form of my letter. The acceptance came in the form of your acknowledging your agreement. The consideration for the agreement is the one hundred dollars to be paid for the services rendered.

Consideration is a very elusive concept. An easy way to think of it is that it is the "tit for tat", the "quid pro quo" or to put it another way, it is simply the meat of the agreement. If there is no consideration, then there is no contract. Going back to the example of the house painting, if I wrote you a letter offering to paint your house, but I never stated when I would finish it or what compensation I expected and you simply wrote back saying that those terms were agreeable then that would probably not be a contract because there is no consideration stated.

Let's look a bit more closely at the three essential elements of a contract: the offer, the acceptance and the consideration.

The offer may come in two different forms. It may come in written or oral form. The more precise the terms of the offer then the better off the parties will be in terms of establishing the certainty of their agreement. A common example of an offer is an advertisement that may appear in the newspaper by a car dealer offering to sell a 1998 Toyota Camry for $17,500. Suppose you were to see that advertisement, and then go to the dealership prepared to pay $17,500.00 and the dealer then told you that there were other terms that were not stated in the advertisement; i.e., handling charges, processing fees and other such fees that are to be added onto the $17,500.00. You could rightfully tell the dealer that they made an offer to sell this vehicle for $17,500.00 and you are prepared to pay $17,500.00 then and there and as such they are obliged to sell the vehicle to you for that amount. Of course on top of that $17,500.00 would be any taxes that are mandated by law. That advertisement, however, constituted an offer and you accepted the offer for the agreed upon consideration of $17,500.00.

If, on the other hand, you had come into the dealership and rather than offering $17,500.00 you offered to pay $17,000.00 for the vehicle, then that would be a counter offer. A counter offer is by its very terms a rejection of the original offer. The dealership of course would be free to reject your counter offer.

There are several different ways that an offer may be framed. That is the person making the offer may state certain terms and conditions that have to be met in order for the offer to be accepted. If those terms and conditions are not met, then there cannot be a valid acceptance of the offer.

Most of us have probably had the experience of attending an auction. The conduct of an auctioneer is similar to that of negotiating a contract. That is, the auctioneer is putting a product on the market for sale and by announcing certain figures, he is requesting offers to purchase that item for that price. If you raise your hand and offer the number that the auctioneer has mentioned, then that is deemed to be an offer for the consideration as stated by the auctioneer. When the auctioneer drops the gavel on the highest offer, that is deemed to be an acceptance of your offer. As part of any auction, there may also be certain published conditions that are made part of the auction. If that is so then by bidding at the auction, you have agreed to those terms.

Contracts are the foundation upon which our economic system is built. They are of such importance that there has developed a body of law known as the Uniform Commercial Code which is a uniform law that has been adopted by most states in the Union either in whole or in part which lays out certain principles dealing with commercial transactions; i.e., contracts. The Uniform Commercial Code in large measure governs the conduct between merchants and other parties dealing with merchants and also governs transactions involving security instruments and negotiable instruments. A security instrument is a document that is typically filed at a courthouse or other public repository which is designed to put the public on notice of the fact that particular items of personal property that may be found at a particular location are security for a debt of the owner of that property to another person. A security instrument in that regard is much the same as a mortgage on your home. A mortgage is a type of security instrument that is designed to secure the mortgage lender in the event you do not make your monthly mortgage payments. If you fail to make your monthly mortgage payments, then the lender has the right to foreclose and to sell your property at public auction. The Uniform Commercial Code (referred to as the UCC) also deals with negotiable instruments. A negotiable instrument is any instrument that may be negotiated or sold for value. For instance, a promissory note wherein one person promises to pay another a fixed amount of money is a negotiable instrument. Likewise, a check is a negotiable instrument. The Uniform Commercial Code deals with the law governing those types of instruments.

As mentioned above, contracts may be either in writing or they may be oral. Whether the contract is oral or in writing, it is equally valid although there may be problems with enforceability as to certain types of contracts that are not in writing. Most states have adopted in some form or another a law know as the "Statute of Frauds". The Statute of Frauds is a law that is designed to minimize the possibility of fraudulent behavior in regards to certain types of transactions. For instance, a person buying or selling land cannot enforce a contract of sale for land unless that contract is in writing. The logic behind that requirement is that over the years there has been so much litigation relating to oral contracts for the sale of land and allegations being made of fraudulent behavior in regards to those actions that it has been found that the best way to minimize potential fraud is to require that those types of contracts be in writing and be signed by the person against whom the agreement is being enforced. That type of requirement is designed to minimize the likelihood of there being any fraud perpetrated against that person. Obviously if the seller signs the agreement and agrees to sell the land for a certain price and all of that is confirmed in writing, then the chance of that transaction being fraudulent is considerably reduced. Other types of transactions that typically need to be in writing are transactions which involve pledging the credit of another for that transaction, agreements to marry, agreements to pay real estate brokerage commissions, agreements that cannot be performed within one year and agreements to lend money or extend credit for an amount of $25,000.00 or more. All of those types of transactions are ones which over the years have been found to be the subject of frequent litigation with allegations being made of fraud. Because of that, many states have found it best to require those types of transactions be reduced to writing and signed by the party against whom enforcement of the contract is being sought.

There are several other defenses that can conceivably be asserted to a claim to enforce a contract. For instance, if one of the parties was a minor or suffering from mental incompetency at the time, then those may be defenses to the validity of the contract. Likewise, if there was a mutual mistake by the parties, then that could void a contract on the theory that there has been no meeting of the minds and therefore no agreement. An example of a mutual mistake might arise in a circumstance where the seller offers to sell his 1964 Cadillac which is parked in front of his home and the purchaser agrees to buy the 1964 Cadillac parked in front of the home. However, it turns out that there were in fact two 1964 Cadillacs parked in front of this home and the parties were referring to different vehicles when they entered into what they thought was their agreement. In that type of circumstance, there has been no meeting of the minds because the parties were mutually mistaken as to which vehicle was being sold.

It is not unheard of that in the course of defending a contract claim, the defendant may claim that he was induced to enter into the contract due to fraud on the part of the other party. Fraud can be loosely defined as a misrepresentation of a material fact. For instance, if I put my home on the market and you respond to my advertisement and come to my home and conduct your own inspection and ask whether I have ever had a wet basement and I tell you that I have never had a wet basement even though I know full well that it is untrue then that misrepresentation may constitute fraud. If you then proceed to buy the house, based upon my false representation and find out after the sale that in fact the basement does leak and has leaked for years, then you may sue me for fraud which induced you to enter into the contract and thereby caused you to suffer certain damages in terms of a mortgage and other closing costs. In the alternative, you may file suit to rescind the contract and ask that all monies that you have paid be returned to you.

Other conceivable defenses to a contract claim could come in the form of duress or undue influence. Duress is simply a threat or perceived threat to induce a party to enter into a contract. Obviously if I put a gun to your head and make you sign a contract to buy my home, that type of contract is not going to be enforceable because you were operating under duress. Duress may come in a number of other forms which may be considerably more subtle. Undue influence arises where certain persons may have a great deal of control over a party and they utilize that control in order to unduly influence a person to enter into the contract. For example, if I hold a power of attorney for my next door neighbor who is ninety four years of age and that power of attorney authorizes me to conduct all of the financial affairs of that neighbor and I then encourage that individual to sign a contract selling his home to me for $100,000.00 under market value, that would be an example of undue influence and would be a basis for setting aside that contract of sale.

If you have ever read a multi-page contract drafted by an attorney, you probably found it to be a nightmarish experience. Although complicated business transactions call for contracts that are precise and by definition complex, most contracts can and should be brief and straight forward. To the extent that there is any ambiguity in a contract, typically that ambiguity is going to be interpreted against the party that actually drafted the contract.

Terms within the contract that are not expressly defined typically are going to be given their dictionary definition by any court that may be called upon to interpret the contract.

A rule of evidence that is important in regards to contract interpretation is the parol evidence rule which states that statements made by the parties prior to the signing of the contract are not going to be considered by a court in a contract dispute. That rule is well recognized and may be further strengthened by language within the contract itself which expressly says that the parties are only bound by the terms of the contract as set forth in the four corners of the document that they have signed. The logic behind the parol evidence rule is that we do not want parties to be relying upon those pre-contract statements to define the intent of their agreement when, in fact, they have gone to the pains of reducing their agreement to writing with the understanding that the writing constitutes the entire agreement. The parol evidence rule may seem to be somewhat inconsistent with the example I gave above of how a party was fraudulently induced to enter into a contract for the sale of a home. The parol evidence rule, however, should not be confused with that instance of fraud. Fraudulent statements that are made to induce a party to enter into a contract are not deemed to be governed by the parol evidence rule; i.e., those fraudulent statements may be a basis for setting aside the contract because those fraudulent statements undermine the integrity and fairness of the agreement.

Once a contract has been entered into, the parties are obviously interested in the performance of the contract. It is not unusual, however, that there are certain conditions imposed on one or both parties before performance is necessary. For example, in your typical homeowner's insurance contract a condition that you must satisfy before your insurance company is obliged to make any payments to you, is to provide a sworn proof of loss statement itemizing the damage that you are claiming. The insurance company also has the right to examine you under oath as to that claim. Once those conditions have been satisfied then the insurance company has an obligation to pay you for the damages incurred which are covered by your policy. Sometimes those conditions within the contract may be the subject of what is referred to as waiver or estoppel. A condition may be waived if the insurance company informs you that you that you do not have to comply with that condition. A waiver is a relinquishment of a known right. If the insurance company has a right to require that you file a written proof of loss and they expressly waive that or tell you that you do not have to file a written proof of loss, then that constitutes a waiver of that condition. In some instances, a party may be estopped from requesting that the conditions be satisfied. For instance, again referring to the insurance claim, if the insurance adjuster handling the matter told you that he would complete the proof of loss form and then submit it to you for your signature within the time allowed by the contract and you relied upon that representation, then the insurance carrier may be estopped from denying coverage to you for failing to have filed the proof of loss form within the time allowed. An estoppel arises, essentially, when a party makes a representation and the other party relies upon that representation to his detriment. In the above example, the insurance adjuster represented that he would complete the proof of loss form, you relied upon that and as a result of that adjuster's failure to do what he said he would do your proof of loss form was not submitted in a timely fashion. In that circumstance, the insurance company would be estopped from denying your claim for failing to comply with the condition.

Just as contracts are the foundation of our commercial system, breaches of those contracts likewise to some extent are the foundation stone of our commercial system. A contract is an agreement. If the agreement is violated then the person who is in violation is liable for the damages called for under the contract. If I agree to paint your house for a hundred dollars and after completing the job satisfactorily you refuse to pay me, then you are in breach of the contract and I can sue you for one hundred dollars. If I have to hire an attorney to file that lawsuit then I may be able to recover my attorney's fees provided that the contract allows for that. The general rule of law in the United States is that each party has to pay his own attorney fees regardless of who prevails. There has been a movement over the last several years to require that in civil litigation the losing party pay the attorney's fees of the winning party. This is in fact the law in some countries. The United States has never adopted that rule because it has been felt that such a rule would deter worthy litigants from bringing claims that are justifiable if they thought that there was any chance of their losing and thereby having to pay the attorney's fees of the opposing party. Referring back to the house painting example, if I knew that you were going to hire the most expensive lawyer in town to defend your good reputation and I knew that those attorney fees could be thousands of dollars that certainly would be a significant deterrent for me to file suit if I thought that I may have to pay all of your attorney fees if I did not win the lawsuit.

The philosophy within our judicial system is that we always want to make the courts accessible to any party who feels as though he has been wronged by some other person. In earlier times, when one person wronged another there might be a duel in the street to resolve that dispute. Our civilization has evolved to the point where obviously we wish to deter those types of confrontations and instead encourage parties to resolve their disputes in a civil fashion in front of a judge or jury. As such the "American Rule" which does not allow for the recovery of attorneys fee unless stipulated in a written agreement is generally considered to be the more democratic rule in that the threat of attorneys fees being awarded is no longer a deterrent to a potential worthy litigant bringing a law suit.

In determining whether one party has failed to comply with the terms of the contract to the point where damages should be awarded, the Court will ask whether the breach of the contract is material. A material breach of contract is one that goes to the very heart of the agreement. In the house painting example, the failure to pay the one hundred dollars obviously goes to the very heart of the agreement and that failure to pay clearly would be a material breach of contract. If, on the other hand, the painter was one day late in completing the job then, typically, that one day delay would not be a material breach of contract unless the contract contained a "time is of the essence" clause. If such a clause was in the contract then that means that the parties have expressly agreed that every minute counts and if the party that is required to perform does not perform on time then that will be considered to be a material breach barring any right to payment that the parties may have.

The damages that may be provided in a contract action generally fall into two categories: direct damages and indirect damages. Direct damages are the damages that are actually spelled out in the contract. In the painting example, the $100.00 that was to be paid would be the direct damages. If, on the other hand, suppose I told you when I agreed to paint your house that I needed to be paid by a certain date otherwise my landlord was going to evict me from the premises from which I operate my business and I then would not be able to operate any further. If that had been disclosed initially and it was within the contemplation of the parties that I would suffer significant consequences if payment was not made in a timely fashion then those consequential damages; i.e., the damages flowing from the failure to pay may likewise be recoverable in a contract claim as indirect damages.

Another form of damage that may be recoverable as part of a breach of contract claim is what is known as liquidated damages. Liquidated damages are damages that are expressly set forth in the contract in the event there is a breach. For instance, in many construction contracts it is expressly agreed by the parties that if the contractor does not complete the job by a certain date then he will have to pay damages of a fixed amount per day. Liquidated damages are frequently called for in contracts because it may be difficult for the parties to determine what the actual monetary damages are in the event of a breach or, in this case, a delay in performance and as such the parties agree to clarify that so that they all know what the consequences will be if, in fact, the contract is not performed in the time frame agreed to.

Claims for breach of contract, aside from involving claims for money damages, may also involve claims for equitable relief. Equitable relief consists of requests by one party to enjoin or dictate either the performance or non-performance of certain things. Suppose I enter into a contract with my neighbor to allow a sewer line to be placed across my property so that my neighbor can hook up to the sewer line. However, when the sewer company comes to install the line I decide to stand at the boundary with a shotgun in my hand to prevent the excavation. In that instance I may be enjoined from that conduct; that is, the Court may order that I step aside and allow the excavation to be completed pursuant to the agreement. The Court in that case would issue an injunction requiring me to cease and desist any behavior that obstructs the excavation. In addition, my neighbor could also sue me also for money damages since I caused him to have to hire an attorney to file a suit for the injunction against me. In that circumstance the attorney's fees might be recoverable.

In reviewing a written contract, there are several things that you need to be on the lookout for:

1. The identity of the parties: Each of the parties needs to be expressly identified. If you are dealing with a corporate entity, then you need to make sure the complete name of that corporation is stated in the contract. The only way to confirm that you have the complete name of that corporation is to call the state agency that supervises corporations to get the complete name. In addition, the contract should expressly identify the position of the person signing

on behalf of the corporation so that it is clear that they are a corporate officer and therefore have the authority to sign.
2. Consideration: The consideration must be expressly stated in the document.
3. Governing law: It is a good idea to state in the contract what state law is going to control this contract in the event there is a dispute that arises. This is important if in fact you are entering into a contract with a person or entity that is not based in the same state where you are.
4. Time of the essence: A time of the essence clause is significant if you are interested in prompt performance by the other party. If prompt performance is not a big deal to you, then you may not want a time of the essence clause. If there is a time of the essence clause in the contract and either party does not comply with the time requirements set forth in the contract, then that is considered to be a material breach of the contract.
5. Survival: The term survival means that if one party to the contract were to pass away before there has been complete performance, then the obligation set forth in the contract would apply to the estate and/or heirs of that person.
6. Modification: It is a good idea to expressly state in the contract that any modification of the contract must be in writing and must be signed by both parties. That eliminates any possibility of there being any oral modification which may be the subject of later dispute.
7. Waiver: A waiver is an intentional relinquishment of a known right. If you waive strict performance of the contract provisions as to the other party on one occasion, does that then constitute a waiver of future breaches by that other party? The answer is it may. Therefore, it generally is a good idea to have a waiver or what I refer to as an anti-waiver clause in

the contract that says that the failure of either party to insist upon strict performance of any of the provisions of this agreement shall not be interpreted as a waiver of any other default or breach of the same or similar nature.

8. Severability: This term means that if any provision within the agreement is found to be invalid or unenforceable it will not effect the enforceability or validity of the other provisions in the agreement. Suppose for instance that a particular paragraph in your contract was determined to be either unenforceable or illegal by a court, that conceivably could invalidate your entire contract unless you have this clause within the contract.

9. Assignability: The general rule is that any contract may be assigned unless the contract expressly says otherwise. Assignment of a contract essentially means that you are selling your rights under the contract to another party. For instance if the contract that you entering into is a contract for the purchase of an automobile, then you may sign a written contract agreeing to buy that automobile for a certain price and then you may assign it (sell it) to another party unless the contract says that assignment is not allowed. What you are selling in this instance is the contract, not the car. You need to decide whether or not you want a non-assignment clause within your contract.

10. Integration: An integration clause in a contract says that this contract contains the entire understanding of the parties and that the parties expressly agree that there are no oral or written representations, warranties or agreements that they have relied upon other than what is expressly said within the written agreement. You may recall that we had previously talked about the parol evidence rule which is a rule of evidence that bars the admissibility of any pre-contract discussions that may have taken place

between the parties before the contract is actually signed. An integration clause reconfirms that and actually goes a little bit further to confirm also that any post contract discussions (discussions or communications that took place after the contract was signed) are not to be relied on by the parties. The word "integration" in this context means that the entire understanding of the parties is integrated into the one document.

B. **TORTS**

A tort is a civil wrong that is not based upon a contract. An example may help clarify that definition. If I punch you in the nose because you say some bad things about this book that I have written then you could sue me civilly for the tort known as battery. In addition, you could go to the local magistrate or the police department and seek to have me arrested for the crime of battery. If you were to sue me civilly, then that would be a civil suit brought in your name against me in the appropriate courthouse. If a criminal prosecution were to be initiated as a result of that battery then that would be a criminal action brought in the name of the government against me for having committed the crime of battery. You would not technically be a party to that criminal prosecution but you would be the main witness or otherwise referred to as the complaining witness.

There are several different types of torts. The most common tort that you may have some contact with is that of negligence. Negligence is a failure to exercise ordinary care. In the definition of a tort, as stated above, I mentioned that it is a civil wrong that arises from a non-contractual basis. If you and I enter into a contract and you breach the contract I can sue you civilly for that breach of contract. The claim that is being asserted there is simply a breach of contract claim. If on the other hand, I run a red light and while running that red light strike your vehicle which is lawfully in the intersection then you could sue me civilly for my negligence in having run the red light. That negligence claim is a tort action that does not arise out of any contract between you and me.

The concept of negligence is founded upon the idea that a duty is owed from one person to another and a breach of that duty which then causes an injury or damage to the other party. For instance in the red light example, the duty that I owed was the duty of not running a red light. If I violate that duty by running the red light and as a result of that you are injured then all of the elements of a negligence claim have been met.

The essential elements of any tort claim are fourfold: There must be a duty that is owed by the defendant (the party against whom the claim is made) to the plaintiff (the party bringing the claim); there must be a breach of that duty or violation of that duty by the defendant; that breach of duty must have then been a proximate cause of injury to the plaintiff; and then finally there must be actual injury or damage to the plaintiff. We have already discussed briefly the first two elements of any tort claim; i.e., duty and breach of duty.

The third element of any tort claim is that of proximate cause. Proximate is not to be confused with the term "approximate". Proximate literally means immediate to, contiguous, touching or direct. Approximate means the opposite. A proximate cause of an event is one which is reasonably foreseeable. If I run a red light then it is reasonably foreseeable that I may injure someone and as such my negligence may be a proximate cause of injury. Let's take another example. Suppose I am playing a game of catch with my son in front of my house and my wind up is perhaps a bit too aggressive and I overthrow the ball. The ball goes through the front window of your home and then through the rear window of your home striking a barbecue stove which is on your back porch which then falls off the back porch, rolls down the hill and strikes your neighbor. The first question is whether I was negligent? I probably was negligent for allowing the ball to be thrown so hard as to break the front window of your home. The next question is whether that negligence was a proximate cause of injury to your home. Clearly it was. The final question is whether or not that negligence was a proximate cause of injury to your neighbor.

That is a tougher question. It comes down to essentially an issue as to whether it was reasonably foreseeable that by throwing the ball as hard as I did that it would not only go through the front window but also the back window and then strike your barbecue oven, knock it off the back porch which would then cause it to roll down the hill and strike your neighbor. That type of resulting injury is probably not reasonably foreseeable and as such the chain of causation would have been broken at some point in that sequence of events. Typically, in that type of case, the question of proximate cause would be submitted to a jury for resolution as to whether or not my negligence was a proximate cause of injury to your neighbor.

The fourth and final element of any tort claim is that of damages or injuries incurred. The issue of damages will be discussed at the end of this section.

Probably the most common form of tort claim that is asserted are claims arising from automobile collisions. Those tort claims normally involve some careless or reckless act by one person resulting in a collision with another motor vehicle. Whether the operation of a motor vehicle involves actual negligence is going to depend upon how the driver's conduct is viewed in the light of the Rules of the Road as set forth either in the State code or the local Code governing traffic regulation. The Rules of the Road or traffic regulations establish the standards for operation of motor vehicles. A violation of these rules or regulations typically constitutes negligence.

Motor vehicle accidents involving common carriers (buses, taxis, trains, planes) may have a set of rules that are slightly different than what would apply in a motor vehicle accident case. Common carriers are frequently held to a very high degree of care. As such, if there is even slight negligence on their part that contributes to the injury of one of their passengers, then the common carrier may be liable.

Another area of the law that produces many tort claims is that of premises liability. A person who is lawfully on someone else's premises and who is injured as a result of some negligence of that property owner may have a basis for a claim against that property owner. The duty or standard of care to which the property owner is held may depend on the status of the injured person. The different statuses that may apply are that of invitee, licensee or trespasser. An invitee typically is someone who is coming onto the property for some legitimate business purpose. A licensee may generally be thought of as a social guest. A trespasser is someone who is not allowed on the premises and who is there without the knowledge or consent of the property owner. Exactly what duty is owed by the property owner to each of these different classes of persons may vary dramatically from state to state. The general rule of law however is that a property owner has a duty to exercise ordinary care to keep his premises in reasonably safe condition. When an owner fails to exercise that ordinary care and someone who is lawfully on the premises is injured as a result of that, then the property owner may be liable. One thing that distinguishes premises liability claims from other types of tort claims is that the party who is injured (the plaintiff) must prove that the property owner had notice of the defective condition on the premises. For instance, if you slip and fall on a liquid that is on the floor in the local supermarket, do you necessarily have a basis for a claim against the owner of the supermarket? You may not unless you have some evidence of how long that liquid had been on the floor. If it turns out that the liquid had only been there a short period of time and is there because of the actions of some other customer in the store and therefore the property owner did not have a reasonable opportunity to see the liquid and clean it up then there may not be any negligence on the part of that property owner. The logic of this rule is that a property owner is not necessarily a guarantor of the safety of all persons on his premises but is simply required to exercise ordinary care. Obviously he can only exercise ordinary care as to those defects or deficiencies that he has some knowledge of or that he should have known of. In that same example, if you were able to prove that the liquid had been on the floor for twenty minutes, then that may be sufficient to make out a claim against the property owner because within that period of time it could well be argued to a jury that the property owner should have known that the liquid was on the floor and therefore should have cleaned it up or placed signs out to warn customers of the presence of the wet floor.

Let me give another example of a premises liability claim that could potentially have some merit. Suppose you are the tenant in a large apartment building where there have been a series of crimes committed resulting in serious personal injuries to the occupants. The property owner is aware of those crimes yet takes no steps whatsoever to warn other tenants of the crime wave in that building and likewise takes no steps to improve security in the building. If you are then subsequently assaulted and injured as a result of a person coming onto the premises for the purpose of committing a crime then you may have a claim against that property owner based upon a negligence theory. That is, the property owner knew or should have known that there was a danger to the tenants yet the property owner took no steps to either warn the tenants or to decrease the security risk to the tenants.

Let's look at that claim from the point of view of how the four elements of a tort claim apply. The first element of a tort claim is the establishment of a duty owed by the defendant to the plaintiff. The duty in this case arises out of the relationship of the parties. That is, the property owner or the landlord owes a duty of reasonable care to persons who are lawfully on the premises. You may ask what is reasonable care? Quite frankly, reasonable care is essentially whatever a jury says it is. A textbook definition of reasonable care is that degree of care that a prudent person would exercise in that circumstance. If the landlord in this instance failed to take some steps to warn the tenants or persons lawfully on the premises of the criminal incidents occurring, then that may be evidence of a breach of the duty to exercise reasonable care. If in fact the assault in question was perpetrated by some person who was unlawfully on the premises then the third element of a tort claim has been met in that that breach of duty has been shown to be a cause of injury. The final element of a tort claim is simply that of injury or damage. In this case, the injury or damage consists of the personal injury to the plaintiff.

Another type of tort claim is a product liability claim. A

product liability claim is one wherein a person contends that a particular product is defective in some way and that defect has produced injury to that plaintiff. You may have some recall of a famous product liability claim that was brought against Ford Motor Company many years ago relating to their Pinto automobile. Ford made an engineering decision to place the gas tank on the Pinto in the rear of the vehicle even though they knew that the placement of the gas tank in this location would result in serious injury to the occupants if the vehicle was involved in a rear end collision. Documentation was produced during that litigation that established that Ford knew or should have known of that risk yet made a conscious decision to continue to keep those vehicles on the road because they felt that the overall financial benefit would weigh in their favor even though they recognized that they would have to pay several million dollars in claims as a result of injuries. The jury in that case returned a very substantial award against Ford Motor Company for compensatory damages for the injuries suffered by the plaintiff in that case and also awarded punitive damages to punish Ford for its wrongful conduct in not taking the vehicle off the road or warning the public of the dangers associated with that vehicle.

Another fairly well known product liability case that has received a good deal of press coverage involved a McDonald's restaurant. In that case, an elderly woman purchased a cup of coffee from a drive-in window at McDonalds and then apparently placed that cup of coffee between her legs and subsequently spilled the coffee. The case received a good deal of attention because it was touted by the insurance industry as being an example of a runaway jury verdict. In fact, the insurance industry failed to disclose to the public that in that particular case the <u>plaintiff</u> had made an attempt to settle the case for simply her medical bills which were substantial because she was hospitalized for over a week. McDonalds however, refused to entertain any reasonable settlement offers. The evidence that was presented at trial was that McDonalds had been warned on many occasions that their coffee was approximately twenty degrees hotter than what was recommended by the local health department and was so hot that it could cause third degree burns. In fact the coffee served by McDonalds was not just hot (135 to 140 degrees) but at a 180 to 190 degrees was able to cook through all layers of skin within seven seconds. McDonalds admitted that its coffee was 40 to 50 degrees hotter than is fit for human consumption and knew that more than seven hundred people, including babies, had been burned by its coffee. McDonalds, however, refused to reduce the temperature of its coffee because it felt that it sold more coffee at that level than it would at a lesser temperature. The plaintiff in this case was an elderly woman who suffered third degree burns over six percent of her body. The state where that case was tried was a comparative negligence state and as such the jury having found the plaintiff partially negligent in terms of how she carried the coffee reduced her verdict by that proportion which was due to her own negligence. The jury in addition to awarding a compensatory damage amount also awarded punitive damages against McDonalds equal to its gross receipts of two days of coffee sales in order to teach it a lesson. The actual verdict in that case was $200,000.00 for compensatory damages and $2.7 million dollars in punitive damages. The punitive damage award was reduced by the court on a post trial motion to $480,000.00. As a result of that verdict, McDonalds reduced the temperature of its coffee. That case was a product liability case in that the theory of recovery asserted by the plaintiff was that McDonalds was negligent in selling a product (coffee) that was defective (i.e., too hot).

A product liability claim may be founded upon negligence principles but it may also raise a legal theory known as breach of warranty. Within the sale of a product there is either an express or implied warranty that the product is reasonably fit for the purpose for which it is sold. If it turns out that the product is not reasonably fit for that purpose then that may constitute a breach of warranty and may give rise to a claim for damages if someone is injured as a result of that breach of warranty. Breach of warranty claims technically are contract claims although they may be asserted as part of a product liability lawsuit.

Normally in a product liability claim the plaintiff will need to present some expert testimony as to what the defect is in the product. For instance, in the Ford Pinto case the plaintiff in that case had to present expert testimony from engineers to establish that the placement of the gas tank in the rear of the vehicle was dangerous and was not good engineering.

Professional liability claims are another form of tort actions that may be asserted. Professional liability claims may come in the form of medical malpractice actions, legal malpractice actions or architectural malpractice actions. In many states the medical profession has been granted certain special protections. For instance some states have imposed a cap or a limitation on the amount of money that can be recovered against any doctor or health care provider as a result of their negligence. The theory behind that cap on damages is to help hold down the cost of medical malpractice insurance coverage for health care providers. In addition, some states have imposed special requirements that must be met before a doctor or a health care provider can be sued. For instance, in some cases the plaintiff must have the claim reviewed by a medical malpractice review panel which then makes a preliminary determination as to whether the claim has any merit. The decision rendered by the medical malpractice review panel may in some instances be admissible in evidence if the case is tried in front of a jury.

A professional liability claim is different from any other type of tort claim that may be asserted because within these types of claims the plaintiff has to typically present testimony from a witness who has some expertise in that field as to what is the standard of care that should have been adhered to by that professional person and then present evidence as to the breach of that standard of care and how that breach caused damage to the plaintiff. In a medical malpractice action, that testimony likely comes from another medical doctor in the same field of expertise as the defendant that is being sued. The same concept applies normally in legal malpractice actions and also in architectural malpractice actions. There could be some instances wherein expert testimony would not be necessary because the negligence is so obvious that there is no need to bring an expert witness into court to explain the technical aspects of the case. For instance if a patient goes into the hospital for an operation on the right knee and the doctor ends up operating on the left knee, obviously there is no need for expert testimony to establish that the standard of care is that the doctor should have operated on the right knee. Any reasonable person would know that the operation on the left knee was unnecessary and therefore was negligent on the doctor's part.

You have all probably heard of the term "attractive nuisance". That is a concept of negligence that is recognized in many states. An attractive nuisance is an object which by its very location and configuration is attractive and also dangerous to children. If the owner of that object allows it to remain accessible to children knowing that it will attract them and knowing that they probably will be injured if they come in contact with it, then that may be a basis for a negligence claim against the owner of that object.

Many tort claims that are brought involve children. Children, in general, are given a favored status in the law meaning that they have special protection. This is true likewise in regards to tort claims. For instance, in regards to negligence claims, children under 7 years of age generally are legally incapable of committing any act of negligence. Children between the ages of 7 and 14 are generally presumed to be incapable of committing negligence although that presumption can be rebutted with the presentation of evidence showing that the child is, in fact, capable of committing a negligent act because of his intelligence level, experience level and other factors that may bear on that.

Those of you with some knowledge of Latin may appreciate the term *res ipsa loquitur*. Literally this Latin term means *"the thing speaks for itself"*. Res ipsa loquitur is a rule of evidence that states that a jury may conclude that a defendant is negligent if in fact the plaintiff has been injured (1) as a result of an instrumentality which is in the exclusive control of that defendant, (2) the defendant has or should have exclusive knowledge of the way that instrumentality was used and (3) the injury is one that would not normally have occurred if the instrument had been used properly. To take a textbook example of that, suppose you are walking down the street and a dresser drawer falls on your head. It so happens that the dresser drawer came from the apartment window above and had been placed there by the tenant who was doing some spring cleaning and the tenant accidentally bumped the dresser drawer. Have the elements of res ipsa loquitur been met in that instance? They probably have been in that the dresser drawer was in the exclusive control of the defendant, the defendant had exclusive knowledge as to how the dresser drawer was used and finally the injury is one that would not normally have occurred if the dresser drawer had been used properly. As long as you can prove those basic elements, you probably would be entitled to recover money against that tenant for her negligence.

Within most negligence claims there arises an issue of standard of care. In an automobile accident case the standard of care normally is defined by the traffic regulations. For instance the traffic regulations dictate that you shall not enter an intersection on a red light. That regulation establishes the standard of care by which all persons are bound in terms of passing through an intersection. In other contexts there may be building codes or other state or local codes that may establish the standard of care by which property owners are bound. Those codes can be the basis upon which a negligence case may be founded because they establish the standard of care to which the defendant is held. If the defendant has violated that code then that may be evidence of a breach of duty by that defendant. If that breach then resulted in damage to you then you may have a basis for a negligence claim against that property owner.

The concept of standard of care becomes especially important in certain types of professional liability claims; for instance, medical malpractice claims, legal malpractice claims or architectural malpractice claims. In those types of claims generally the plaintiff has to establish what the standard of care is. The standard of care normally is established by means of the presentation of evidence by experts in that field. For instance, if in the course of your open heart surgery the surgeon happens to penetrate your coronary artery with a catheter and you suffer irreparable damage, has the standard of care for that procedure been violated? That is not something that I could answer as a non-medical person. Nor is it something that you could answer as a non-medical person. Nor is it something that a group of jurors could answer as non-medical people unless they hear evidence from a medical expert establishing what the standard of care is. The standard of care in that particular instance may be that the surgeon through the use of radiological instruments, should have been able to tell where his catheter was going and therefore should have known when he was about to puncture the arterial wall and therefore could have avoided it if he had he been attentive to the radiological instrument that showed him where the catheter was. In that instance, the standard of care evidence presented by the plaintiff may show that the doctor was negligent in puncturing the arterial wall with that catheter. You can probably rest assured that the defendant doctor will bring in his own medical expert who will refute that and who will state that there is no standard of care in this circumstance, that this was simply an unfortunate accident that happened, and that there was no negligence on the part of the doctor.

In addition to proving that there was a breach of the standard of care by a doctor the plaintiff must also show that the breach was a proximate cause of the injury of which the plaintiff complains. For instance in the example of the puncture of the arterial wall by the catheter, the defendant may argue that even if that was negligence the patient only had a 5% chance of survival and therefore he probably was going to die anyhow and, as such, any negligence that may have been committed was really irrelevant. This is a frequent defense raised in professional negligence claims and is frequently one that has some merit; i.e., the doctor may have been negligent, but the patient would have died anyhow. This reemphasizes the importance of the concept of proximate cause. That is, even though the doctor may have been negligent, the negligence may not have been a cause of injury since the patient may have suffered that injury in any event.

Another concept within the field of negligence that occasionally receives some popular attention is the concept known as strict liability. Strict liability means that the defendant is liable for his conduct in certain instances without a showing of actual negligence if that conduct was a cause of injury to the plaintiff. Strict liability normally only arises in regards to activities that are extremely dangerous. For instance, if you are operating a quarry and in the course of blasting with dynamite you damage the home of one of your neighbors, that neighbor may not have to prove that there was any negligence on your part in the blasting operation but simply has to prove that the blasting was the cause of damage to his home. In that circumstance, the party conducting the blasting may be strictly liable for any damage that results from that dangerous activity. This is a principle that is applied in certain circumstances such as blasting and other types of activities that the law may deem to be inherently dangerous.

Different states have different ways of how they deal with negligence claims in that some of them acknowledge the concept of comparative negligence while other states are known as contributory negligence jurisdictions. In a comparative negligence jurisdiction, the negligence may be compared between the parties. For instance, going back to the red light example, if I ran the red light and struck you while you were in the intersection but you happened to be intoxicated and laying in the middle of the intersection due to that intoxication then there obviously would be some negligence on your part. The jury would be called upon to compare the different levels of negligence. For instance in that example they might conclude that I was 50% negligent and you were also 50% negligent for being intoxicated and laying down in the middle of the intersection. If the jury then determined that your total injuries were $100,000.00 you would only receive $50,000.00 because you were 50% negligent.

In a contributory negligence jurisdiction there is no comparison of negligence which means that if you were negligent even by 1% and that negligence was a cause of your damage, then your claim is barred and you receive nothing. Contributory negligence is a principle derived from the common law which is still recognized in some states. It is indeed a very harsh principle of law and in many instances works an injustice to people who are probably entitled to recover something for their damages but may not be entitled to 100% compensation.

There are several affirmative defenses that may be raised in regards to a tort claim. An affirmative defense is a defense that may be raised by a defendant that constitutes a complete bar to a claim. One of those affirmative defenses is that of the statute of limitations. Every state has set forth a statute of limitations for virtually every type of civil claim whether it be a tort claim, contract claim or otherwise. If the claim is not asserted within the time allowed by that statute, then the claim is deemed to be barred. The assertion of a claim is accomplished in most states by actually filing the law suit at the courthouse. Some state require actual service of the suit papers upon the defendant before the statute of limitations runs.

Another defense that may be asserted in a tort case is that of assumption of the risk. Assumption of the risk involves the plaintiff understanding the nature of the risk involved and a voluntary acceptance of that risk. For instance, if you decide to go out to the supermarket during the middle of a very bad ice storm recognizing that the roads and walkways are not navigable and while walking from your car to the store, you slip and fall, then you probably have assumed the risk since you obviously knew that there was a risk associated with going out during those weather conditions and you voluntarily chose to accept that risk.

Several states still recognize various types of immunities. That immunity may come in the form of sovereign immunity, charitable immunity or family immunity. Sovereign immunity is based upon the concept that the King cannot be sued; i.e. the sovereign or the government cannot be sued. Many jurisdictions have waived that immunity either in whole or in part. If the local or state governmental entity that you are planning on suing is deemed by state law to be immune from tort claims, then you may not be able to sue that entity at all unless they expressly choose to waive their immunity. Many governmental entities by means of state law have expressly waived their immunity either entirely or have allowed claims to be asserted against them up to certain dollar amounts. This is something that varies from state to state.

Charitable immunity is a doctrine that applies in many states to organizations that are truly charitable. A charitable organization is generally considered to be one that fulfills strictly a charitable function and does not make any attempt to collect its debts. Charitable organizations may be immune from tort claims. For instance, if you were injured on the premises of the Red Cross because of some negligence on their part, depending on the law in that particular state where the Red Cross building is located, the Red Cross may well be subject to the defense of charitable immunity because they truly are a charitable organization.

There are certain states that still recognize elements of family immunity; that is, tort claims may not be asserted against parents or siblings for certain types of behavior.

A concept within tort law that is of significant importance is that of vicarious liability. The concept of vicarious liability essentially means a principal may be liable for the conduct or the misconduct of his agents. That principal/agent relationship arises in the employment context between an employer and an employee. It may also arise in other contexts involving contractors. From a plaintiff's point of view the concept of vicarious liability is important because it typically is that legal concept that allows for complete recovery of damages. For instance, if you are rear ended by a truck driven by an employee of the ABC Company, your attorney in filing a suit would file the claim against not only the driver but the also the employer. If suit was filed only against the driver and it turns out that there was no insurance covering that vehicle, then whatever judgment you got against the driver may be uncollectible simply because the driver may not have the financial resources to pay the judgment. If, however, you get the judgment also against the employer, then that employer probably would have the financial resources either in the form of insurance coverage or otherwise to satisfy the judgment. The employer in that case is liable for the conduct of the employee assuming that the employee was acting within the scope of his employment. If, on the only hand, the employee was off on a personal mission of his own while operating a company vehicle and the employer had no knowledge of that and had not consented to it, then there may not be any vicarious liability in that sense because the employee was off acting on his own and was not doing anything on behalf of the employer at the time of the collision. The concept of vicarious liability has been the subject of a good deal of litigation over the years. For instance, suppose an insurance salesman comes into your home to sell you insurance on behalf of the XYZ Company and he presents to you his business card along with all the brochures of the XYZ Company and convinces you that based upon the extensive advertising of that Company and because of the well recognized name that this is a very reputable company to deal with and based upon that you purchase a policy of insurance and tender a check in a substantial amount. If the salesman then absconds with the money, is the XYZ Company liable for your loss? They probably are even though that salesman may not be a direct employee of the company. The salesman in that instance may be an independent contractor but the XYZ Company is still probably going to be liable because they are the ones who gave that salesman all the trappings of authenticity, gave him the opportunity to engage in his fraudulent behavior and essentially set the whole process in motion through the use of its company name and company advertising.

An important principle in terms of liability in a tort action is what is known as joint and several liability. For instance, if I run a red light and strike you in the intersection and the vehicle that I am driving belongs to my employer then I may be liable for that act of negligence and my employer may also be liable. The liability that is imposed there is known as "joint and several" which means that the plaintiff could sue me alone or could sue the employer alone or could sue both of us and whatever judgment the plaintiff gets against us could then be collected by the plaintiff against me solely or against the employer solely or against either one of us to the extent that we have assets to pay. Under the principle of joint and several liability each defendant is 100% liable for the judgment that is rendered. That is a principle that has been under a good deal of attack lately because it can create circumstances wherein a defendant can wind up paying more than his fair share of any judgment especially if the other defendant cannot afford to pay. Joint and several liability is something that is well ingrained into our legal system and the rationale behind it is to make sure that the Plaintiff can obtain at least one full recovery for whatever judgment is entered. It then becomes the burden of those defendants against whom the judgment has been entered to fight among themselves as to any eventual sharing of that liability.

Aside from the types of claims mentioned above, there are several intentional torts that can be asserted. Those intentional torts consist of such claims as assault and battery, conversion, defamation, false imprisonment, fraud, malicious prosecution, invasion of privacy, trespass and the intentional infliction of emotional distress. All of these claims have specific elements that must be met and proved in order for a plaintiff to prevail.

A battery is simply an unwanted touching of one person by another. Conversion is the taking of a person's property without that person's consent. Defamation can come in either written (libel) or oral (slander) form and consists of making injurious statements about a person that are untrue. If those injurious statements involve an imputation of a criminal offense, involve moral turpitude, impute a contagious disease, impute unfitness to perform the duties of office or words that prejudice a person in his profession or trade then they may be referred to as being defamatory per se. If the alleged statement is not defamatory per se, then the plaintiff may have to prove what are called special damages in order to recover against the defendant. Special damages would come in the form of out-of-pocket expenses incurred as a result of those defamatory statements. For instance, if you are a surgeon and I call you a butcher, that is a statement that is defamatory per se and therefore you could assert a defamation claim against me even though you may not have incurred any special damages; i.e., any out-of-pocket expense as a result of my making that statement. If, on the other hand, you are unemployed and I call you a butcher, and as a result of making that comment you incur so much emotional distress that you seek psychiatric help then you may likewise have a basis for a defamation claim against me. Even though the comment made is not defamatory per se, the fact that you have incurred medical expenses as a result of my making the comment about you satisfies the special damages requirement and therefore gives you the basis for a defamation claim against me.

Claims of false imprisonment and malicious prosecution arise in the context of a person improperly restraining another person or initiating a criminal prosecution which is subsequently found to be unjustified.

As mentioned above, fraud is the intentional misrepresentation of a material existing fact made for the purpose of inducing reliance and which in fact does induce reliance to the detriment or damage of the plaintiff. Fraud is a very difficult thing to prove. Unlike most civil claims which must be proven simply by a preponderance of the evidence or what is referred to as the greater weight of the evidence, fraud claims must be proved by clear and convincing evidence which is a much higher standard therefore making it much more difficult to prove. The reason for the higher standard of proof in regards to fraud claims is that the law recognizes that fraud is an offense that involves surreptitious behavior that may be subject to different interpretations. It is therefore felt that the plaintiff should have a more difficult burden of proof in regards to these types of claims than would apply in regards to the run of the mill tort claims that may be asserted.

The final element of any tort claim that must be established is that of damages. Damages may also be thought of as the injury incurred. The injury may come in the form of personal injury such as a broken arm or leg, pain and suffering, emotional distress, medical expenses, lost wages and/or permanent disability. Those are all potential elements of damages that may be claimed in a tort action.

If the injury suffered results in the death of the plaintiff, then that person's estate may assert what is known as a wrongful death claim. A wrongful death claim is a claim wherein the injured party rather than having simply suffered personal injury has actually died as a result of the misconduct of the defendant. A wrongful death claim may be based upon a negligence theory, a breach of warranty theory or based upon an intentional tort theory such as assault and battery. Wrongful death claims are a fairly recent phenomenon in that the common law did not recognize wrongful death claims on the theory that once a person had died obviously there was no amount of money that could compensate him. As such, his claim died with him. The state legislatures, however, over the years have come to recognize that even though death may bring an end to the suffering and damages incurred by the decedent there may be persons left behind who have been damaged and may continue to be damaged in the future as a result of the passing of that person. Every state has its own wrongful death statute and that statute will define exactly what damages are recoverable under the wrongful death act. Typically the damages recoverable are damages consisting of solace and grief experienced by the survivors, loss of earnings suffered by the dependents left behind as a result of the death of the decedent and his subsequent inability to generate income, any medical expenses incurred by the decedent in his last illness and the funeral expenses.

C. **DOMESTIC RELATIONS**

The field of domestic relations law is sometimes loosely referred to as divorce law. Domestic relations, however, covers much more than simply entry of a divorce decree. It covers such things as the award of custody of minor children, the payment of spousal and child support and the distribution of property in the event of a divorce and adoption.

Let me begin by talking about some principles relating to marriage and the termination of a marriage. There are two types of marriage that may be recognized: A common law marriage and a ceremonial marriage. The law differs from state to state as to whether or not common law marriage is recognized. A common law marriage is a marriage wherein a couple have lived together for the required period of time (typically seven (7) years) and have publicly held themselves out to be husband and wife. They may do that by not only sharing the same household and the same bed but perhaps by even sharing the same last name, having children, referring to each other as husband and wife and engaging in all of the typical activities that one might attribute to a married couple. If those requirements are met, then that couple is deemed in the eyes of the law of that state to be married.

A ceremonial marriage, however, is conducted by an authorized minister, justice of the peace or other designated official who has the authority granted by the state to conduct civil marriage ceremonies.

In all states in the Union once a couple is deemed to be married, whether it be by common law or means of ceremony, that marriage may be terminated only by a decree of court. The divorce decree does not necessarily have to be entered in the state where the parties were married. Quite frequently one or both parties may change their residence in order to come within the jurisdiction of another state or foreign country in order to have a "quickie" divorce entered. Those types of divorce decrees may be valid provided there was a bona fide change in residence and provided proper notice was given to the other spouse of the fact that the marriage is to be terminated. You could very well have a situation where a couple is married in the state of Massachusetts, one spouse moves to Nevada for the purpose of having a divorce decree entered. The other spouse while residing in the state of California then challenges that divorce decree on the grounds that the other spouse did not in fact take up a bona fide residence in Nevada or on the grounds that there was improper service or notice of the suit given to the party residing in California.

A divorce may be decreed either on fault grounds or no fault grounds. The fault grounds for a divorce are adultery, constructive desertion, cruelty and actual desertion. The no fault basis for a divorce is that there is no attribution of fault to the other party but simply that the parties have lived separate and apart for the period of time required by state law with the intent to terminate the marriage.

Adultery is the act of engaging in sexual relations with a person other than your spouse during the marriage. Obviously that is a rather difficult thing to prove. It is rare that the offending spouse is actually caught "in the act". More often what the jilted spouse does is to have the offending spouse followed by private detectives who then photograph or otherwise record the conduct of the offending spouse going to the home of the paramour, spending the night there and then exiting the following morning. The court will generally accept that as evidence of the fact that an illicit affair is going on.

Desertion is the intentional departure from the family home without the consent of the other spouse. Constructive desertion may exist in an instance where one spouse has made the circumstances within the family home so intolerable as to cause the other party to desert or leave the family home. That conduct may come in the form of abuse, denial of sexual relations or other egregious conduct that essentially results in a termination of the marriage. A final fault grounds for divorce is that of cruelty which comes in the form of mental abuse or physical abuse.

Another means by which a marriage may be terminated is through annulment. Again the grounds for annulment are defined by state law. Those grounds may be such things as lack of capacity due to being under age, fraudulent misrepresentation as to intent in entering into the marriage as evidenced by a failure to ever consummate the marriage, insanity or failure to disclose a prior felony conviction. Annulment is different than divorce in that instead of ending the marriage, the law considers the marriage to have never existed at all.

One thing that distinguishes divorce proceedings from most other types of civil claims is that there generally is a requirement of corroboration of the basic elements of the divorce claim. That is, the parties alone cannot prove the grounds for divorce. Many states require that the testimony of one or both parties be corroborated by a third person in order to establish the grounds for divorce. For instance, in an adultery action, one spouse simply saying that she saw the other spouse actually engaged in sexual relations with a third person is not sufficient to establish adultery. Instead that evidence must be corroborated by a third person. The third person could be the paramour or more often is going to be a private detective. The rationale behind this requirement of corroboration is that the state has an interest in preserving marriage and therefore the parties themselves should not be allowed through their own testimony or evidence to terminate the marriage. Although there has been a movement over the years to liberalize the basis for divorce throughout the United States, in some areas of the country that movement is seeing a reversal where some states are actually trying to make it more difficult for parties to divorce; i.e., by providing a longer waiting period before a divorce may be decreed.

Many states still recognize divorce actions in the form of a divorce <u>a mensa et thoro</u> and divorce <u>a vinculo matrimonii</u>. A divorce <u>a mensa et thoro</u> is literally a divorce from bed and board which is a type of legal separation that may continue until the final decree of divorce is entered in the form of a divorce <u>a vinculo matrimonii</u> (from the bonds of matrimony). That final decree of divorce is entered after the statutory separation period has been satisfied or in some cases based upon some fault grounds such as adultery. A divorce <u>a mensa et thoro</u> enables the parties to get a legal separation when they are unable to get a full divorce due to religious or other circumstances.

The party against whom a divorce action is brought may raise certain defenses to that claim. Those defenses may consist of such things as condonation, consent, justification, laches, reconciliation and recrimination. Condonation is very simply the act of forgiving the marital offense. For instance, if a husband learns that his wife has engaged in adultery and thereafter takes her back to the marital bed, that is deemed to be a condonation of the marital offense of adultery. Likewise, if one party consents to the other party leaving the marital home, that is a defense to a desertion claim. If one party has engaged in egregious conduct that justifies the departure of the other spouse from the marital home, that may constitute justification. Laches is a type of statute of limitations defense although it is not governed by an express code section that sets forth a precise period of time within which a claim may be brought. You may recall earlier that we talked about law claims and equitable claims. Divorce actions are deemed to be equitable claims because typically the parties are not suing for an express monetary amount, but rather they are asking the court to award certain forms of equitable relief; i.e., the awarding of a divorce, the awarding of custody or the distribution of marital property. If one party sues the other party on fault grounds, but does so after a substantial period of time has elapsed after the fault conduct occurred and as a result of that lapse of time the other party is prejudiced due to the loss of witnesses or loss of evidence then that may give rise to the defense of laches. Another defense that may be raised is reconciliation which is essentially the fact that the parties have gotten back together. Recrimination as a defense may be applicable where the spouse bringing the claim has herself likewise engaged in conduct that may be the basis for divorce and that constitutes a defense to the claim.

Although the core of most domestic relations work is that of obtaining a final decree of divorce, there are many additional facets to domestic relations work. If there are any children of the marriage then, as part of that final decree of divorce, the court will have to award custody to one or both parties and typically will fix monetary amounts for child support awards and spousal support awards if necessary.

Years ago many courts recognized a presumption in regards to custody issues that favored the mother; i.e., she was presumed to be the more appropriate parent to whom custody should be awarded. The father would then be awarded visitation rights which would mean that he could have the children in his physical control at the times allowed by terms of the court decree. Other than those visitation rights, the father frequently had no other rights. For instance, a father typically would not even have the right to talk to the children's teacher in order to inquire as to how they were doing, be involved in their sports activities, or even have access to their medical records. In the last several years custody arrangements have typically been liberalized so that a more common arrangement is an awarding of joint legal custody which means that each parent retains full parental rights to be involved in the lives of their children although one parent will be granted primary physical custody of the children. The other parent then will have custody (or what otherwise might have been referred to as visitation) during designated times that are established by the court or agreed to by the parties.

Where custody is contested between the parties, the court will look at a number of different factors in deciding which parent should have primary physical custody. Those factors may include such things as the employment status of the parents, their capability of providing for day care, the amount of spare time that the parent will have to be involved in the lives of the children, whether a change in custody would involve uprooting the children from their school and neighborhood, the financial status of the parties, any mental or emotional difficulties manifested by either party and to some extent the wishes of the child depending upon the age of the child. The older the child is the more likely it is that the court will entertain evidence as to what the wishes of the child may be.

Aside from actual parental custody, grandparents to some extent may have rights as far as visitation. The right of grandparent visitation normally is not going to be to the detriment of either parent but typically will be allowed during the period of time when the related parent has actual physical control of the child.

It is not unusual after a final decree divorce has been entered that the non-custodial parent files a motion with the court requesting a change of custody so as to award him or her primary physical custody of the child. Such a motion is generally based upon there having been some material change in circumstance affecting the interests of the child. The general rule of thumb that the court applies in terms of awarding custody is to determine what is truly in the best interest of the child. The court certainly would look at any and all of the factors mentioned above plus any number of other factors that may be pertinent. Once custody has been awarded to one party, it generally takes some fairly egregious conduct on the part of the custodial parent or some significant change in circumstance in order to justify a change in custody. The prevailing wisdom is that even though the current arrangement may not be perfect, children do tend to crave stability in their lives and therefore the court must hear some fairly compelling evidence before it will change that otherwise stable arrangement.

Other issues that a domestic relations court may be called upon to decide are those relating to adoption and legitimacy of children. An adoption procedure again is strictly governed by state law. The court supervises that adoption procedure in order to ensure that the new adoptive parents are fit and appropriate persons to have custody of this child. The procedure involves an initial review of the adoptive parents before they actually receive the child. Then there is a period of time when the child will be allowed to be with the parents on an interim basis. Finally the entire situation will be reviewed again before a final order of adoption is entered. Once a final order of adoption is entered then the adoptive child acquires the same status as a natural child of that couple.

Another issue that may arise in the course of domestic relations litigation is that of legitimacy or paternity. If in fact a man has fathered a child, then the mother has a right to claim child support from the father. If the couple is not married, then there may be an issue as to parentage. That is fairly easily resolved through blood testing. Once parentage is established, then the father or non-custodial parent will be ordered to provide child support based upon his or her income level and the needs of the child.

In awarding child support either in a divorce action or in a paternity action, the court looks at several factors in determining what the amount of that support will be: the respective income of the parties, the financial needs of the parties, whether the parties are fully employed or are underemployed. Many states now have statutory guidelines as to child support amounts. Those guidelines are published in the state code and they are based upon the gross income of the parties. A formula is then applied in order to determine exactly what amount of child support is due from the non-custodial parent.

Either party to a divorce action may also make a request for spousal support or what has traditionally been known as alimony. This is something that may be claimed by either the husband or the wife. The general rule of thumb is that the principal bread winner in the family is obliged to maintain the other party in the style of life to which they have become accustomed during the course of the marriage. As a practical matter, that frequently is not possible. If a couple was living on $45,000.00 a year before the divorce and the husband is the sole breadwinner in the family, then once they divorce there obviously is going to be a reduction in lifestyle.

The distribution of property acquired during the course of the marriage is another issue that a domestic relations court is called upon to resolve as part of a divorce action. The distribution of property can become very complicated in instances where you are dealing with pieces of real estate, stocks and bonds that have appreciated in value or pension and retirement plans. These frequently require an analysis by a CPA or an economist to determine what the total value of those various assets are and then recommendations to the court as to how each party has contributed to the increase in value of those assets and what the total value of the assets are. For instance, if the parties have been married for 20 years and if during the course of that marriage the husband was employed at all times by AT&T and he is due to retire a year from now, does the wife have some interest in his pension? The general answer to that question is yes. Does that mean that she gets one half of all of his pension payments? That again is going to be governed strictly by state law but the general factors that are going to be looked at are how much of the pension eligibility years coincided with the years of the marriage, what was the actual contribution of each party to that marital asset and to what extent were pre-marital assets utilized to acquire what now is deemed to be a marital asset.

Frequently parties avoid court involvement in terms of a distribution of property by entering into a pre-nuptial agreement prior to the marriage or by entering into a property settlement agreement after the parties have agreed to separate. An ante-nuptial agreement is an agreement that sets forth what the entitlement will be of either party in the estate of the other in the event of a divorce. These types of agreements are becoming more and more common especially in second marriages. A property settlement agreement is an agreement or a contract entered into by a husband or a wife after they have agreed to separate that sets forth the terms of any property distribution, custody arrangement and support obligations.

The tendency in some states is to endeavor to streamline divorce litigation mainly for the purposes of preserving the court's time and the court's resources. In the state of Virginia, obtaining a divorce decree can be a very complicated endeavor. If the parties are proceeding on fault grounds, then typically that case will be referred to a Commissioner in Chancery, a local lawyer who conducts a hearing or mini-trial wherein the parties appear with their witnesses and exhibits and their attorneys and they present their evidence in support of their claim for fault grounds for the divorce. That Commissioner then prepares a written report to the Circuit Court Judge recommending whether the divorce be granted; and if so, whether on fault grounds or no-fault grounds. The parties may then have to appear before the Court for trial in order to litigate issues relating to child custody, child support and the distribution of property. The Court at that same time reviews the report from the Commissioner in Chancery and can either accept or reject the findings made by that Commissioner as far as the grounds for the divorce. The divorce process in Virginia therefore can be a two stage proceeding; i.e., first appearing for a Commissioner's hearing in regards to the grounds of the divorce and then appearing before a Circuit Court Judge to resolve the other issues in the case.

D. <u>CRIMINAL LAW</u>

The distinguishing feature of criminal law is the element of punishment. The purpose of the criminal law is to punish wrongdoers. If someone is accused of a crime and subsequently convicted of that crime, then they are to be punished. That is dramatically different than the purpose of civil law. Civil law generally is intended to compensate someone for an injury they have suffered or to undo a wrong that has been committed. In the field of criminal law, the victim is not necessarily compensated but the perpetrator is to be punished. In the eyes of our criminal justice system, the purpose of that punishment is to help reform the perpetrator, to restrain future misconduct by that perpetrator, to create a system of deterrents as to other potential perpetrators and finally to obtain retribution for the crime that has been committed.

The ultimate punishment allowed in our criminal justice system is that of capital punishment. That form of punishment is reserved for the most heinous crimes.

The material of which many mystery novels are made is homicide, sometimes referred to as murder. There are different degrees of murder. The premeditated, willful and deliberate killing of another is "murder one" or capital murder. If I set out to kill you, and then in fact do kill you with the intent to kill you, then that constitutes murder in the first degree. If on the other hand I kill you in the heat of an argument and there is no element of premeditation, then that may qualify as murder in the second degree. If I am simply negligent and as a result of that negligence you are killed that may be negligent homicide. Felony murder arises where any death results during the commission of a felony. A felony is a crime for which a person can be imprisoned for more than a year. A misdemeanor is a crime for which a person can be imprisoned for up to a year. Many jurisdictions make distinctions as to whether this type of murder will be murder one or murder two depending upon the type of felony that is being committed.

A rule that applies in many jurisdictions to this day is the so called "year and a day" rule which means that a death cannot be attributed to the defendant's wrongful conduct unless the death occurs within a year and a day of that conduct. So if the person died after a year and a day of the wrongful conduct, then the defendant could not be charged with murder.

Murder is the most significant crime against a person. Other crimes against a person are such crimes as battery, assault, mayhem, forcible rape, kidnapping and robbery.

There also several crimes that are classified as crimes against property. One of those crimes is that of larceny which involves the taking and carrying away of the valuable personal property of another with the intent to permanently deprive the person of that property. If I walk into a department store and pick up a coat off the rack and walk by several cash registers and then walk out the door with the intent of not paying for the coat, then I have committed larceny. If on the other hand, I simply walk out of the store in a moment of forgetfulness with the coat in my hand not realizing that I had not paid for it, that is not larceny. I may however still be arrested and charged with larceny.

Embezzlement is a property crime that is defined as the fraudulent conversion of the property of another by a person who has lawful possession of the property. If an employee of mine removes money from my cash drawer and converts that money to his own personal use, then that person has committed embezzlement. Embezzlement normally involves someone who is in a position of trust who has access to the money or property of another. False pretenses is also a property crime. False pretense is defined as obtaining title to property by knowingly or recklessly making a false representation of a presently existing fact of monetary significance which is intended to and does defraud the victim. False pretenses is very much like the civil claim of fraud.

Another property crime is that of forgery. The most common instrument that is involved in forgery is that of a check. If I have insufficient funds in my banking account and I write a check on that bank account is that forgery? The answer to that is no. The check I wrote is genuine. Forgery is the false making or altering of a legally significant instrument (for instance a check) with the intent to defraud. A related offense is that of uttering. Uttering consists of negotiating or attempting to negotiate an instrument which I know to be false. The term uttering literally comes from the fact that words are "uttered" in presenting that document for negotiation.

Receiving stolen goods is another property crime. To be guilty of receiving stolen goods, the receiver must know or believe the goods were stolen. Extortion is a property crime which involves the making of threats for the purpose of obtaining money or property. If I threaten to expose you as a philanderer unless you give me a thousand dollars, that may be extortion. Another property crime is that of burglary which consists of breaking and entering the structure of another for the intent of committing a crime. Normally the crime that is intended to be committed is that of theft or larceny; i.e., removing something from the premises.

There are a multitude of other property crimes.

An essential element of a criminal offense is what is known as *mens rea* or intent. Different crimes may require different levels of intent. There are a variety of different ways that the courts have addressed these levels of intent. Two common distinctions albeit somewhat confusing are that of specific intent and general intent. A specific intent crime is one that calls for a particular state of mind in order to satisfy the elements of that offense. For instance in first degree murder, there must be premeditation; i.e., a specific intent to kill. In second degree murder however there need not be a specific intent to kill. There may simply be a general intent. A person who kills another with a gun while voluntarily intoxicated to the extent that he is unaware that he even has a gun would be guilty of second degree murder.

Another aspect of intent is what is referred to as transferred intent. Transferred intent arises where a person intends to harm one victim but in fact harms another. If I throw a rock at you and rather than hitting you, I hit your next door neighbor I may still be guilty of the crime of assault and battery even though I did not intend to hit your neighbor. My intent is deemed to be transferred from you to the neighbor.

In the field of tort law, we talked about strict liability and vicarious liability. To some extent those concepts are also recognized in criminal law. Strict liability arises where a conviction can be obtained merely upon proof that the defendant perpetrated an act forbidden by statute. A type of strict liability offense is a traffic violation. If you run a stop sign, it makes no difference what your intent was. The mere act of running the stop sign makes you guilty of a violation. Vicarious liability can arise also in the criminal context when the conduct of another person can be attributed to you. For instance, if I run a restaurant and an employee of mine sells alcohol to a minor, then I may be liable under the local liquor laws.

Aside from intent, another essential element of most criminal violations is that of *actus reus* meaning the guilty act. If I merely form the intent to kill someone but never do anything to actually implement it, then I have not committed any crime. If however I form the intent and then I go out and purchase the weapon and enter into a conspiracy to use that weapon to kill someone then I may be guilty of a crime. In order to constitute *actus reus* it must be a voluntary act. These two critical elements of *mens rea* and *actus reus* must occur concurrently. For instance, if I intentionally shoot to kill you but miss and later accidentally kill you, am I guilty of murder? The answer is no. Because at the time that I committed the act (*actus reus*) I no longer had the intent *(mens rea)*.

We have talked above about several different types of crimes. A subsidiary form of criminal behavior is that of the attempt to commit a crime. An attempt to commit a crime normally involves a specific intent. For instance, attempted murder involves the specific intent to kill. If my intent however is only to cause serious bodily harm, then I cannot be guilty of attempted murder. Because attempt requires a specific intent, it is impossible to attempt a crime which by definition cannot be committed intentionally. For example, involuntary manslaughter cannot be attempted because it requires the wrongdoer to cause death <u>unintentionally</u>.

Another type of criminal behavior is that of solicitation. Solicitation involves a specific intent to engage in a particular type of criminal conduct. If I tell another person that they ought to burn down city hall, that would not constitute solicitation. However, if I tell another person that he must burn down city hall <u>now</u>, that may be solicitation.

The law also recognizes principals and accessories in criminal activity. The getaway man (driver) in a bank robbery who does not actually go into the bank is an accessory and he probably is as guilty as the principals who were actually in the bank. If, however, I am not even at the scene of the bank robbery but I assisted the bank robbers in getting the car that was to be used as the getaway vehicle knowing that it was to be used for that purpose, then I may be an accessory. An accessory in that context probably would not be subject to the same punishment as a principal. I could also become an accessory by assisting the bank robbers in eluding the police in which event I would be an accessory after the fact. Again in that type of circumstance, I probably would not be subject to the same punishment as the principals. More difficult cases arise in instances where a person is present at the time of a crime under circumstances that suggest approval. Normally this is not sufficient to convict a person of a criminal violation. One exception to this would be an instance where the defendant is under a duty to act. If a father stands by idly while his minor son attacks a third person then, at least in some states, he could be guilty of a criminal violation.

Prosecutors over the last several years have become more daring in bringing conspiracy charges against persons involved in criminal behavior. Conspiracy is an agreement between two or more persons to commit an unlawful act or to commit a lawful act in an unlawful manner and one or more person makes an overt act in furtherance of the conspiracy. In a conspiracy case, the agreement itself is the actus reas and the intent to commit the unlawful act is the mens rea. Suppose you and I agree to attack a third person with our fists but during the course of the attack I wind up shooting the third person, are you liable for my act of shooting that third party? Probably not unless you knew or should have known that I had a gun. If you knew or should have known that I had a gun, then you may be liable for my conduct because you should have known that the aggressive behavior that we set out on could lead to my shooting someone.

There are several defenses that can be raised in a criminal case. One of the more newsworthy defenses is that of insanity. Different states have adopted different rules as to how insanity is to be determined. Some states adopt a simple right/wrong test known as the M'Naghten rule which simply is a determination of whether the perpetrator was able to distinguish right from wrong. Other states adopt the so called "irresistible impulse" test which may apply in an instance where a defendant knew he was doing wrong but the status of his mind prevented him from controlling his conduct; i.e., he was overtaken by an irresistible impulse to engage in that behavior. The District of Columbia adopted the so called Durham test several years ago which provides that an accused is not criminally responsible if his unlawful act was the product of mental disease or mental defect. These types of insanity defenses are generally the subject of a good deal of controversy and normally involve expert testimony from psychiatric witnesses.

Another defense that can be raised is that of intoxication. If a crime requires specific intent, then a person who is intoxicated may be incapable of forming that specific intent. Other defenses that may arise are that of coercion, necessity and entrapment. Coercion arises in instances where there is duress. The bank teller who turns over the bank's money to the robber is acting under duress in doing so and therefore is not guilty of larceny in removing the money from the drawer. A woman who is threatened with sexual assault who then breaks down a neighbor's front door to seek refuge is not guilty of burglary because her conduct is governed by the defense of necessity. Entrapment is a much more difficult defense. The purpose of the entrapment defense is to prevent the government from manufacturing a crime. An undercover police officer who offers to purchase narcotics at the going price from one whom he believes to be a pusher is not guilty of entrapment. An undercover police officer, however, who applies immense pressure to a suspect to sell him narcotics by establishing a friendship with him and then playing on that friendship to overcome that person's unwillingness to sell narcotics probably would be guilty of entrapment.

Another defense that may be raised to some criminal violations is that of vagueness. The U.S. Constitution precludes punishing a person under a statute that is too vague to be understood. That is, the statute should be sufficiently clear that a reasonable person could determine what conduct is forbidden and the statute should be sufficiently clear as to prevent arbitrary enforcement by the police. Loitering statutes over the years have been subject to tests for vagueness. Indeed, if they preclude any person from congregating on a public street essentially at any time, then they may be subject to constitutional challenges for vagueness.

The ultimate defense to a crime against a person is that of self defense. As a general rule a person may use whatever force is reasonably necessary to prevent immediate and unlawful harm to himself. Some jurisdictions have adopted the so called retreat rule which requires a person who can safely retreat to do so before using deadly force. Can the defense of self defense come into play in a circumstance where a person is subjected to an unlawful arrest? Theoretically it may although, as a practical matter, resisting an unlawful arrest is a risky maneuver because that could result in worse physical harm to you. In general, the defense of self defense does apply so as to permit a person to employ reasonable non-deadly force to resist an unlawful arrest. Although the defense of self defense only applies to crimes against the person, a related defense in property crimes is that of protection of property. As a general rule, a person can use whatever force, short of deadly force, that reasonably appears to be necessary to protect property. A classic case in that regard involves the homeowner who laid a trap in his home consisting of a spring gun which then fired when the burglar entered the front door. If at the time of the shooting the homeowner was not home, then that homeowner may be criminally liable.

E. **LANDLORD TENANT**

The relationship between a landlord and a tenant is governed by a contract. That contract is referred to as the lease. A lease is an agreement between the landlord and the tenant wherein the landlord agrees to allow the tenant to occupy a building or a piece of property owned by the landlord in return generally for the payment of periodic rent. As such any issues relating to landlord tenant law must initially be looked at in terms of what the lease calls for as to the respective rights and obligations of the two parties.

The specific terms of the lease however may be superseded by either local or state law. Many local and state governments have enacted landlord tenant legislation. Landlord tenant laws normally only apply to residential leases. A residential lease is a lease between a landlord and an individual who intends to occupy that space as his residence. A commercial lease on the other hand is a lease between a landlord and a tenant who occupies the space for business or commercial reasons. The landlord tenant laws typically do not apply to a commercial lease.

Landlord tenant laws may come in a variety of different forms involving such things as rent control, the obligation of the landlord in terms of dealing with security deposits, the obligations of the landlord in terms of maintaining the premises and a multitude of other such related issues.

In order to fully ascertain what the respective rights and obligations are of the parties to a lease, you must first look at the lease itself and then determine whether there are any local or state statutory provisions that may override or supersede any provisions within the lease. For instance if a landlord in renewing a residential lease chooses to increase the rent but the pertinent rent control law precludes such an increase in rent, then that law will supersede the terms of the lease that may have been agreed to and the landlord can obtain no more than what the law allows as far as rental. Likewise, if the lease provides that the landlord is not responsible for maintenance of the premises, that too may be superseded by the landlord tenant law that applies in that jurisdiction which expressly imposes the obligation upon the landlord to maintain the entire premises in a reasonably habitable condition. Indeed many such landlord tenant laws not only impose that obligation on the landlord but also give the tenant the right to actually abate or reduce the rent if in fact the tenant has to incur expenses in order to make the premises reasonably habitable.

The scope of the law governing the landlord tenant relationship may be further expanded by case law interpreting the landlord tenant law of that jurisdiction.

A lease, being a contract, is subject to all of the comments made previously in the section on contracts. In addition there are several provisions within a lease which both parties need to be sensitive to:

1. <u>Destruction</u>: The lease will frequently set forth the rights of the tenant if the premises should be destroyed by fire or other catastrophe. A fairly typical provision in this regard would to be to allow the tenant to declare the lease null and void if the premises cannot be restored to their prior condition within sixty days. Obviously the tenant does not have to pay rent during the period of time when the premises are not habitable. Such a provision however may be highly detrimental to the tenant because it may obligate him to occupy the premises on the sixtieth day assuming they are restored to their prior condition. That is not much solace to the tenant if in fact he has no place to live or to run his business during this sixty day period.
2. <u>Subletting</u>: Frequently a lease will bar subletting. This may be important from the landlord's point of view because the general rule of law is that any contract (including a lease) can be assigned unless there is a provision within the contract that says it cannot be assigned. An assignment simply means that one party to the contract may assign or sell his rights to a third person. In the case of a tenant, the subletting of the premises is an assignment of the tenant's rights to a third person who would then have the right to occupy the premises in lieu of the tenant who signed the lease. If the lease, however, precludes that then subletting may be prohibited. Certainly from a landlord's point of view such a prohibition is desirable because the landlord wants to know with whom he is dealing.
3. <u>Uses</u>: The lease should expressly state what the intended uses of the premises by the tenant are and confirm that these uses do not in anyway violate any condominium association regulations, homeowner's association regulation or zoning regulations.
4. <u>Taxes, utilities, insurance and condo fees</u>: The lease

should indicate who is responsible for payment of these.
5. <u>Security deposit</u>: The lease should expressly indicate what the amount of the security deposit is, who is holding it, is it being held in an interest bearing account and how much time the landlord has after the termination of the lease in order to make an accounting for the security deposit.
6. <u>Obligations and rights of the parties</u>: The lease should indicate exactly what the respective obligations and rights are of the landlord and the tenant. Things that should be addressed are the right of access of the landlord, the right of the tenant to make alterations, the need for smoke detectors or carbon monoxide detectors and the use of any heavy equipment or electrical items that may overload the system.
7. <u>Subordination</u>: If the owner of the property is liable on a mortgage or deed of trust as to the property then it is prudent for the owner to state in the lease that the lease is subject and subordinate to all mortgages and deeds of trust, the tenant agrees to sign all documents upon the request of the landlord confirming such or in the alternative the landlord is authorized to sign such documents on behalf of the tenant. This issue would only come into play if the premises were going to be refinanced or sold and the lender required some confirmation that, in the event of a foreclosure, their right to foreclose would not be impeded by the existence of tenants on the premises.
8. <u>Joint liability</u>: If there are two or more tenants on the lease then it should be expressly stated in the lease that the tenants are jointly and severally liable. That means if there is a default or a breach by the tenants then the landlord can collect 100% of the money due on the lease from either one or both of the tenants.

F. ESTATES

The law dealing with estates is that body of the law that deals with the estates of people who have passed away as well as people who during their life either voluntarily or involuntarily have conveyed their property to a third person for purposes of managing that property.

Let's deal with the law of decedents first. This general area of the law is sometimes referred to as probate. The term probate literally means "to prove". What is going to be proved in this instance is a Will. A Will is a written statement signed by a person indicating their wishes as far as the disposition of their assets upon their death. A Will of course never becomes an operative document until that person passes away. Prior to the person's death, the Will may be amended at any time assuming that the person is competent. The objective of a Will is to provide for an orderly transfer of assets from one generation to the next. If a person dies without a Will, then the transfer of his or her assets will be governed by the law of intestacy. The law of intestacy is that body of law established in the state code that dictates who will be the recipient or recipients of the property of a decedent if that person dies without a Will. For that reason it always is preferable to have a Will since that gives you control over how your property will pass. If you do not have a Will, then the law of intestacy will control. That law varies dramatically from state to state but typically it establishes an order of priority which normally would consist of most of the assets going to the surviving spouse and then if there is no surviving spouse then to the surviving children and if no surviving children then perhaps to parents or siblings of the decedent.

If a person dies with a Will, then typically that Will be probated. Probating the Will simply means presenting the Will to the Clerk of the local court that has jurisdiction over wills and estates and proving that it is authentic. Most Wills that are done are self authenticating. What that means is they are witnessed by the number of persons required by state law, notarized and contain the necessary language required by state law in order to make them self proving or self authenticating. If in fact the Will is self proving or self authenticating then all that need be done is to present the Will to the Clerk of the court. The clerk will then accept it upon payment of the proper filing fee. At that point the Will has been probated or proved.

Some states allow handwritten or what are referred to as holographic wills. A holographic will must be completely in the handwriting of the person signing the will. That is, you can't have someone else handwrite a Will for you. If there is any handwriting on the Will other than your own then the Will would be considered to be ineffective. The problem with a handwritten will is that it is not self proving or self authenticating. Your Executor would need to bring witnesses to the courthouse to prove that it is in fact your Will.

Normally within a Will there is a designation of an Executor. The role of the Executor is to gather all of the assets of the decedent, report to the Court as to what those assets are and then supervise the orderly distribution of those assets in accordance with the Will. If a person dies without a Will, then the individual that is appointed for this purpose normally is referred to as an administrator who serves the same general purpose as the Executor; i.e., the gathering of assets, reporting to the court and then eventual distribution of assets.

The process of gathering the assets, reporting to the court and then distributing the assets is supervised by the local court where the Will was probated. Generally there is a court officer who is responsible for that supervision. The purpose of the court supervision is to ensure that the wishes of the decedent are carried out. The administration of estates can frequently take many years depending upon the size of the estate and the terms of the Will, including the administration of any trusts created by the Will. As part of the administration of an estate, normally any potential creditors should be given notice of the fact that the estate is being administered. Those creditors then have a designated time to make claims against the estate. If those claims are not made within the time allowed, then the claims are deemed to be denied and then at that point, the assets of the estate can be distributed.

Within the administration of any estate there may be significant tax consequences. An estate that consists simply of a marital transfer, i.e., from one spouse to another normally does not involve any estate tax consequences. Instead, the tax consequences will occur when that surviving spouse passes away. The objective of this tax law provision is to attempt to ensure that the surviving spouse has sufficient assets during his or her life to maintain himself/herself, but then upon the death of the surviving spouse the estate will be taxed according to the federal estate tax law. There may however be state inheritance taxes that must be considered.

Taxation of property transferred by an individual to others at his death is one of the oldest and most common forms of taxation at least in societies where property is privately owned. Gift taxes and death taxes in the form of estate or inheritance taxes are generally referred to as "transfer taxes". The transfer of property may be in the form of a gift or in the form of a conveyance at the time of death. A federal tax on transfers at death was first employed in the form of an inheritance tax in 1862. At first it applied only to personal property but later it was extended to real property as well. In order to avoid the federal and state taxes on transfer of property at death some property owners made large transfers during their life. To counteract this technique and partly for political reasons the Federal Gift Tax was enacted in 1924.

The transfer taxes were not enacted merely to raise revenue. Indeed overall they do not raise that much revenue. In the year 1992 they accounted for about 11.5 billion dollars of tax receipts. In part they were designed to prevent people from accumulating large blocks of wealth and then transmitting those blocks from generation to generation. Overall the IRS has not been terribly successful in that regard.

In determining federal estate tax liability the first issue that must be addressed is what is the gross estate. The gross estate includes at a minimum the value of all property owned by the decedent at death which passes to somebody else. This includes some life insurance proceeds and some jointly owned property. As such, the gross estate for tax purposes is not necessarily the same as the estate that might be reported to the local court for probate purposes. Once the gross estate has been calculated then there are certain allowable deductions that may be taken to arrive at what is referred to as the taxable estate. Those deductions include allowances for most transfers to a surviving spouse (the marital deduction), contributions to charity and deductions for certain debts and expenses.

The gift tax is designed to be a companion tax to the estate tax. The gift tax applies to any gratuitous transmission of property during a person's life since a transfer of that nature has the effect of reducing the estate subject to estate tax at the time of death. There are certain exclusions in regards to the gift tax. For instance each year a person is entitled to an annual exclusion for gifts in an amount of $10,000.00 to each donee. Only if the amount given is more than that excludable amount in one year to one donee will the gift be taxable.

The property transferred from one spouse to another at the time of death in general is not subject to any estate tax. If the surviving spouse consumes part of what she inherited and holds only about $650,000.00 at the time of her death then she will be able to transmit that property outright without a tax on her estate because the $650,000.00 exemption would apply to that.

In light of that $650,000.00 exemption per person it makes sense to take advantage of that exemption in most instances for each party. In order to do that each party would have to have an estate at the time of death of as much as the exempted amount which is currently $650,000.00. That can be done by means of establishing a marital trust. For instance suppose that the total estate of a couple is 1.3 million dollars. Those total assets could be divided equally between the two parties and placed in trust for each for use during their lifetime after the death of the first spouse. To be more specific suppose the husband passes away first and a marital trust has been established for the benefit of the wife. $650,000.00 would pass to the wife at the time of the husband's death outright. In addition there would be another $650,000.00 in trust that could be used for her benefit under the terms of the trust at the passing of the husband. That $650,000.00 that was held in trust would then pass to the next generation free of estate tax. If on the other hand the entire 1.3 million dollars had passed to the wife at the time of death and assuming that she did not consume any portion of that then her estate would be 1.3 million dollars at the time of her death and therefore would be subject to tax on the amount over $650,000.00. The marital trust in this first instance saved approximately $200,000.00 in federal estate tax.

A few important things to remember about federal transfer taxes are the following:

1. Estates valued in 1998 at under $650,000.00 are not subject to any taxation. The valuation of an estate, however, includes not just assets and properties in existence at the time of death but also the entitlement to certain life insurance proceeds.

2. Assets that are simply transferred from one spouse to another are not subject to federal estate tax at the time of the death of the first spouse but rather they are subject to taxation at the death of that second spouse. There are a number of ways in which the estate tax burden can be reduced because of this. The principal mechanism is the marital estate trust.

A second component of estate law is that which deals with transfers of property either voluntarily or involuntarily from one person to another during that person's life. Such a transfer may come in the form of a trust, guardianship or conservatorship. A guardianship is normally established when a person is considered to be incompetent to manage his or her own personal financial affairs and therefore needs to have a guardian appointed to manage those affairs. In such a proceeding, the local court first determines the person to be incompetent, and then designates a guardian or conservator to manage that person's estate and perhaps also to manage that person's life. The guardian then becomes the decision maker for that person in all aspects as allowed by the court order. If the court order authorizes the guardian to completely control the assets of that person then those assets are to be managed in the method deemed best by the guardian. The guardian must act in the best interest of the person who has been declared incompetent (the ward or the beneficiary) and the guardian must report to the court on a periodic basis as to where the assets are and, to the extent that they have been expended, what they were expended for. A frequent instance where you see a guardianship created is in a circumstance where a parent becomes too elderly or infirmed to manage his or her own affairs in which event the children may request the court to have a guardian appointed who will then manage the parent's financial and personal affairs.

Another way to accomplish this same objective of guardianship is through a durable power of attorney. The durable power of attorney is a power of attorney that continues in existence after a person becomes incompetent and it designates another person as the attorney in fact or the agent of the individual for the purposes of carrying on all of the affairs of that individual. For instance, a spouse who is about to go into serious surgery may sign a power of attorney to the other spouse authorizing the other spouse to sign his name to checks, to convey real estate and to do all acts that the first spouse could do if in fact he was fully competent. A power of attorney is a document wherein one person authorizes another person to act in his behalf either generally or for a specific purpose. The advantage of a power of attorney is that it is less formal than a guardianship. The disadvantage of a power of attorney is that it does not involve court supervision and therefore is potentially subject to abuse on the part of the attorney-in-fact.

Another type of conveyance that may be subject to court supervision is that of a trust. A trust very simply is an agreement normally in writing wherein one person (the trustor) conveys property to another person (the trustee) for the benefit of a beneficiary . The trustor and the beneficiary may be one and the same person. For instance I may convey property to my wife in trust for her to use for my benefit in the event I become incompetent and cannot manage my own affairs. In doing so, I have actually conveyed that property to my wife and she then becomes the legal owner of that property but she can only use it for my benefit. Such a trust may be filed with the local court in which event it then becomes subject to court supervision much like a guardianship. On the other hand, the trust in some jurisdictions may not have to be filed in the court in which event it becomes very similar to a power of attorney in that there is no court supervision of how the assets are managed.

G. **TAXES**

Taxes of course are something that we are all familiar with. We can be taxed at the Federal level, state level and local level. Federal tax consists of income taxes and estate taxes. At the state level, taxes may come in the form of income tax, sales tax, inheritance tax and licensing taxes. At the local level, typically the taxes are licensing taxes and personal property taxes although some localities may have the authority to impose income taxes and sales taxes.

The complexity of the tax laws throughout the nation far exceed the scope of this book.

Taxes are generally thought of as a means for the government to generate funding for its operations. Taxes, however, are strongly rooted in social policy. If the sole purpose of taxes was simply to generate money to support the government then a flat tax on income would make perfect sense. A flat tax of perhaps 17% on all income would be simple for the taxpayer and also easy for the government to administer. Such a flat tax, however, would negate any social considerations of encouraging home ownership through mortgage deductions, encouraging charitable contributions through charitable deductions and further would thwart all types of social policies that are an inherent part of our tax code.

At the federal level, the primary tax is that of the income tax. Most of us know this form of taxation by the completion of the annual 1040 form for the IRS. The income tax is a relatively new creation having only been in existence for approximately a hundred years. Prior to that there was no income tax. The income tax is designed to tax anything that is referred to as income or what otherwise might be thought of as economic gain. That gain can come in the form of wages, in the form of profits or gain from the sale of property, earnings from gambling or proceeds from winning the lottery. If you buy stock at a hundred dollars per share and sell it at three hundred dollars per share, then your gain or profit is two hundred dollars per share. That gain is subject to taxation. The amount of tax that you will pay depends in part whether it is subject to long or short term capital gains. Long term capital gains are gains that relate to property that you have held for more than eighteen months and are subject to a lower tax than short term capital gains or profits.

Overall, the amount of tax that you pay to some extent depends upon what tax bracket you are in. Currently there are several different tax brackets that are governed by your overall income level. Whatever income you have may be subject to certain deductions and also to a variety of different credits that may be available. A deduction is simply that; i.e., a deduction against your adjusted gross income. Common deductions are the home mortgage interest deduction, the payment of state taxes, real estate taxes and charitable deductions. These deductions do not reduce your tax burden dollar for dollar. Instead they simply reduce the amount of income that you have that is subject to tax at whatever your tax rate may be.

This is to be contrasted with a credit. A credit is a dollar for dollar reduction of your tax obligation. For instance if your adjusted gross income is one hundred thousand dollars and your total deductions are forty thousand dollars then your taxable income is sixty thousand dollars. At that level of income, your total obligation may be in the range of twenty thousand dollars and if you then have credits that you are entitled to, then those credits will reduce that twenty thousand dollar obligation dollar for dollar. As such, if you have the entitlement to five thousand dollars in credits than your actual tax burden will only be fifteen thousand.

Income that you receive in some instances can be subject to double taxation. For instance, if you are a principal owner of a corporation and the corporation receives income then the corporation may be taxed on that income. If you then distribute that income to yourself as compensation for being an officer or as shareholder dividends then that income may be taxed a second time as your personal income. This double taxation can be avoided by designating your corporation as what is referred to as an "S" corporation. The designation of "S" is derived from subchapter "S" of the Internal Revenue Code.

Another federal tax is the Federal Estate and Gift Tax. These forms of taxation are discussed in the section dealing with estates.

At the state level, taxes may come in several different forms. The state income tax which exists in most states is generally keyed to the federal income tax. The tax at the state level for income is generally considerably less than at the federal level. Other forms of state taxes are the sales tax which is a tax on the sale of all goods. There may also be a number of different state licensing taxes. Those taxes may come in the form of licensing motor vehicles, professional licenses or occupational licenses. Many localities have what is referred to as a business license tax. This tax in some jurisdictions is a gross receipts tax. I like to think of it truly as being an income tax but the local taxing authorities will refer to it not as an income tax but rather as a tax on gross receipts for a business in that locality. Generally the tax rate for this tax is fairly low but it is a tax on essentially every dollar that that business brings in the door irrespective of how much actual income the owner of the business may derive from it. As such, a business may have gross receipts of a $1,000,000.00 and also have expenses of a $1,000,000.00 in which event there is no income generated. That business, however, is still going to pay a gross receipts tax on the million dollars of gross receipt.

The Internal Revenue Service is an agency within the Department of the Treasury. The main office of the Internal Revenue Service is in Washington, D.C.. The regional offices are divided into seven geographic areas. Within each region there are ten service centers which primarily deal with the processing of returns, selections for audit and in-office audits.

In 1988 Congress passed a taxpayer's bill of rights. This bill of rights requires that the IRS inform the taxpayer regarding the determination or collection of tax in simple non-technical terms. Taxpayers are also entitled to notice regarding the procedures for appealing adverse decisions, prosecuting refund claims and filing taxpayer complaints. In addition the IRS must notify the taxpayer of collection and enforcement procedures under the Internal Revenue Law.

A return filed with the Internal Revenue Service may be examined closely or not at all. In most cases the review of the return at the service center is the beginning and the end of the Internal Revenue Service review. Some returns, however, are sent for further examination. A small minority of those returns are then subjected to an audit. If the taxpayer disputes the initial determination of liability in the audit process then the taxpayer may appeal that decision within the Internal Revenue Service.

The theory behind auditing tax returns is to encourage taxpayers to comply voluntarily with the tax laws. The selection of returns for review involves both computer analysis and also a manual inspection of the returns. What the IRS is looking for is those returns with a high probability of error resulting in some significant change in tax owed. These audits may be conducted at the service center or more significant audits may be conducted at the district office. An audit at the district office level may consist of an office audit which typically is performed by tax auditors in an IRS office or it may consist of a field audit which consists of the examining agent making an appointment at a time and place convenient to the taxpayer. At any such audit the taxpayer has a right to have his accountant or attorney present. The possible outcomes of an audit are that there is no change in the tax owed, there may be a proposed adjustment with the taxpayer signing a waiver of notice of any deficiency or in the alternative the taxpayer may simply refuse to accept any adjustments proposed by the auditor. In those contested cases the taxpayer will receive a thirty day letter. This letter entitles the taxpayer to file a written protest to the proposed adjustments to the tax owed. If the taxpayer does not respond to that letter then the IRS will attempt to contact the taxpayer regarding his choice of action. If there is no response from the taxpayer to that then the IRS issues a ninety day letter which is a notice of deficiency. If the taxpayer chooses to protest after receipt of the thirty day letter then the matter may be reviewed by the appeals office within the Internal Revenue Service. Once all of the appeal rights are exhausted at the appeals office level then the

IRS will send a notice of deficiency. If the taxpayer wishes to pursue the matter further then he must take his case to court. Taking a tax case to court means filing a petition before the Tax Court of the United States or the taxpayer may file suit in the United States District Court in the district where the taxpayer resides or with the United States Court of Claims in Washington, D.C. Before the United States District Court acquires jurisdiction over such a claim the deficiency in taxes must be paid by the taxpayer. This is an important distinction between actions filed in the U.S. District Court versus actions filed in the Tax Court; i.e., a tax case filed in the U.S. Tax Court does not require the taxpayer to pay the deficiency before filing the suit. There may be other tactical advantages in filing in one court versus the other depending upon which federal district you live in and which way the wind happens to be blowing at that time as to tax issues in the Tax Court or Court of Claims.

H. **REAL ESTATE**

Real estate law to some extent is similar to contract law in that the underpinning of most real estate transactions is a contract. A contract to sell real estate is an agreement between a buyer and a seller to convey title to a piece of real estate for a given price.

The contract may contain a number of contingencies. A contingency is a provision within the contract which states that the contract may be declared null and void by one or both parties unless certain events occur. For instance, a standard provision within a commercial real estate contract is what is known as a feasibility contingency. The feasibility contingency generally gives the purchaser anywhere from thirty to sixty days to study the property to determine whether it can be used for the commercial purpose that the buyer intends to use it for. The study by the purchaser may involve a review of the zoning laws, studies of the soil to make sure that the land is suitable for the intended construction or engineering analyses to determine that the contour of the land is appropriate for the intended construction. A similar type of contingency is found in a residential contract and it is generally referred to as a home inspection contingency. That home inspection contingency usually gives the purchaser anywhere from five to ten days to have the home inspected to determine whether it meets with the purchaser's approval. At anytime during the home inspection contingency, the purchaser may rescind the contract. Another contingency within most contracts is the finance contingency. That is, the buyer's obligation to settle is contingent upon the buyer being able to get the necessary financing or money from a lender on terms agreeable to the buyer in order to acquire the property. If the buyer cannot do that, then the buyer's obligation to settle on the contract is nullified. Once all of the contingencies have been removed, then the buyer and the seller are irrevocably locked into going to settlement.

A real estate settlement typically consists of the parties appearing either at a lawyer's office or the office of a settlement agent. There the seller signs a deed to the property, the purchaser signs whatever financing documents are necessary in order to obtain the loan and then a variety of other documents may be signed in order to satisfy the requirements of the institutional lender who is providing the money for the purchase of the property and the title insurance company who is insuring that good and marketable title is passing to the buyer.

In going to settlement or going to closing (the terms are generally used synonymously), title to the property is being conveyed from a seller to a purchaser. Title to the property means the ownership interest that is of record at the courthouse or other place where deeds are recorded. The conveyance of title is accomplished by means of a document referred to as a deed. A deed is a written instrument signed by the seller identifying the property in question by precise legal description and stating the nature of the title interest that is being conveyed by the seller to the purchaser. The deed may then be recorded at the courthouse to serve as a notification to the entire world that the seller is no longer the owner of this property but in fact on the date in question has conveyed the property to the purchaser. The conveyance is considered to be effective when the deed is physically delivered by the seller to the purchaser. That delivery normally occurs at settlement when the seller signs the deed and then tenders it to the settlement agent who is acting on behalf of the purchaser.

There are a number of different forms of title ownership that may be conveyed. The most common forms of title ownership are what are referred to as legal title and equitable title. Legal title is determined by looking at the deed to determine who at that point in time is recognized by the deed as being the owner of the property. For instance, in regards to my home which I purchased over 20 years ago, my wife and I are the title owners of that piece of property. When we bought that property over twenty years ago, there was a deed conveying the property to us and we have never sold that property to anyone else. We have however conveyed equitable title to the lender who initially loaned us the money to purchase the property and likewise have since refinanced the property several times and therefore have signed additional documents conveying equitable title to those additional lenders.

Different jurisdictions handle real estate financing in different ways. In some states the real estate financing that is utilized for a purchaser to buy real estate is by means of a mortgage. In other instances, it may be by means of a deed of trust. Although those different documents can have significantly different meanings, the effect is giving a security interest in your real estate to the lender who loaned you the money in order to acquire the property or to refinance the property. If you do not make your monthly payments in a timely fashion, then the lender may decide to foreclose. If they foreclose, then that means that they are going to be selling your property at a public auction where any bidder could come in and bid on your property. The objective of the lender in that instance is to recover all of the money loaned to you which is still outstanding plus any interest that is due at that point along with any expenses, trustee fees and/or attorneys' fees that they have incurred in terms of having to foreclose.

Suppose you buy a piece of property for one hundred thousand dollars and you obtain ninety percent financing meaning that ninety percent of the purchase price is coming from a lender. That means that you would have to put ten thousand dollars of your own money into the purchase in order to go to settlement. At settlement, you will receive a deed from the seller indicating that legal title is being conveyed to you. At settlement, you would sign a mortgage or deed of trust wherein you are conveying equitable title to the lender to secure the $90,000.00 loan. Under the terms of that document, the lender gives you the right to remain in the property and to treat it as your home, but in return you have to make sure that you properly insure the property, properly maintain it and also most importantly make the monthly payments on time. If you fail to do those things, then the lender can foreclose and attempt to sell the property in order to recoup the ninety thousand dollars that may still be outstanding plus any additional cost or expenses that they have incurred. If that property were to go to foreclosure and were to be sold at a public auction shortly after you acquire the property, then it is unlikely that the lender would be able to sell the property for much more than what you paid for it and as such, there probably would be no surplus or excess left in the sale price that would go back to you.

Sometimes in the course of dealing with a piece of real estate there may arise an issue as to who owns that piece of real estate. Every state has their own way of recording ownership interest in real estate. One way of determining who the owner of a piece of real estate is to call the local real estate tax office. The tax office should have a record as to who they report as being the owner of the real estate. Those records are, however, are not always reliable. In order to determine the true owner or owners of a piece of real estate you may have to have a title search done. There are title examiners or title insurance companies that are available to do that for a fee. That is probably the only sure way to determine who all of the owners are of a piece of real estate as of a specific date in time. A title examiner, in determining ownership interest, will check all of the various indices at the local courthouse (or other governmental office building where deeds and land records are maintained) to determine:

1. Who was the last person to have been deeded that

property? This may tell you who the title owner is of the real estate as of that date but it does not tell you whether or not there could be any other persons that might have a right to claim some interest in that property. As such it may be necessary to do a historical search of the chain of title going back many years to determine who all of the other title owners had been.

2. To do a thorough search of the title, it would be necessary to determine whether during the ownership interest of any of the title owners there had been any liens noted of record that might apply to the property. Liens may come in the form of tax liens, mortgage liens, deeds of trust, mechanics liens or judgment liens. If there have been any such liens then it must be determined whether those liens have been properly released of record so that they no longer apply to the property.

3. If any of the title owners passed away during the period of their ownership of the property then it may be necessary to check the Will index to determine whether their Will is of record and if so what their Will indicates as far as the transfer of this property.

Suffice it to say that in many states the determination of the true owners of a piece of property can be very complex. If you are simply interested in general information as to ownership interest reliance upon the tax records may be sufficient. If, however, you are contemplating purchasing real estate or filing a legal action against the property owners it is advisable to have an appropriate title search done of the property to make sure you are acquiring good title or suing the correct owners.

As indicated above, the traditional way by which a person acquires ownership of a piece of property is by means of a deed. There is a principle recognized in real estate law known as adverse possession which is another means by which a person may acquire ownership of a piece of property. If I decide that I would like to use the small lot next to my home that I know is owned by my next door neighbor and I then park my boat on that property and I use that piece of property for my own purposes freely, openly and exclusively then over a period of time I may acquire adverse possession of that property. The period of time for which I must "adversely possess" the property is dictated by state law. Once that period of time has passed and the true title owner has not objected to my use of the property then the law may deem me to be the owner of that property by adverse possession. In order to truly acquire title to that piece of property, however, a suit would have to be filed to have the court confirm that in fact I acquired the property by means of adverse possession.

If you are contemplating entering into a real estate contract, you should have the contract reviewed by an attorney of your choosing. All of the considerations previously mentioned in regards to contracts would be applicable to a real estate contract. In addition some specific things that you should be on the lookout for are the following:

1. Property description: The property must be precisely described. There are different ways of describing a piece of real estate. It can be described by means of a street address. The street address for purposes of a residential contract may be sufficient. However, the so called legal description should also be added. The legal description is the description as set forth in the deed by which the current owner acquired the property. That legal description may frequently be referenced by a subdivision with a section number and a lot number. Another means of describing a piece of real estate is by means of a tax number or tax map number. Many jurisdictions have broken every piece of property down by number for purposes of taxing. Another means of describing a piece of real estate is by what is called a metes and bounds description. Metes and bounds is a description generally given by a surveyor wherein the surveyor describes the entire perimeter of the property in terms of distance and compass directions. It is not

unheard of that people enter into a real estate contract thinking that they are buying one piece of property and in fact they end up taking title to a different piece of property. If there is any doubt in your mind as to what piece of property you are buying then you need to have a survey done and perhaps even meet with that surveyor at the property so that you can actually walk the property bounds.

2. Earnest money deposit: The earnest money deposit is an amount of money that literally is designed to show that the person making the offer to buy the property is "in earnest" about their intent to buy the property. If you make an offer to buy a piece of property for a million dollars but only propose an earnest money deposit of one hundred dollars that tells me that you are not truly in earnest. There is no strict requirement as to how much the earnest money deposit should be but certainly it is not unusual that the earnest money be in the range of five to ten percent of the total contract price. It must be clearly indicated how that earnest money deposit is going to be held. If it is going to be paid by means of check then typically it would be tendered to a real estate broker that is involved in the transaction and then placed in that real estate broker's escrow account. If in fact the contract is finally ratified; i.e, fully accepted, then the contract needs to state who gets the earnest money deposit in the event there is a default by one or both parties. The earnest money deposit will be credited against the total price at settlement.

3. Financing: Most real estate purchases are going to be financed generally by an institutional lender; i.e., a bank or mortgage company. Financing terms (amount being financed, the interest rate, the term of the note such as five years, etc.) should be spelled out in the contract. If there is any financing that is being provided by the seller then that likewise needs to be spelled out. For instance, if the property is being sold for a hundred thousand dollars and the purchaser is obtaining fifty thousand

dollars of that purchase price from a bank and the seller then is going to hold a promissory note for fifty thousand dollars for the balance of the purchase price then that should be spelled out in the contract. The bank's note would likely be secured by a first deed of trust against the real estate you are buying and the seller's note would then be secured by a second deed of trust. The terms of the note to the seller needs to be set forth and the fact that the note to the seller is to be secured by a second deed of trust also needs to be set forth.

4. <u>Contingencies</u>: Within most real estate contracts there is a financing contingency meaning that the buyer's obligation to actually go to settlement is contingent upon the buyer obtaining financing (money for the purchase) from a lender. If the lender rejects the loan application of the buyer then the buyer usually cannot go to settlement. In a typical residential real estate settlement the buyer has to obtain a loan commitment from a lender prior to settlement and upon obtaining that loan commitment the financing contingency may be removed. Removal of the financing contingency, however, is always somewhat dangerous because there are situations that could arise wherein the buyer may not be able to get the financing from that lender. From the buyer's point of view the buyer always wants to have a way of getting out of the contract in the event he cannot get the financing. The seller on the other hand would like to lock the buyer in by having that financing contingency removed at some point in time prior to settlement. Another type of contingency would be a feasibility or inspection contingency mentioned above.

5. <u>Title to the property</u>: Within the contract it must specify that the seller is going to give good title to the property. Title can be conveyed in different ways in different jurisdictions. Typically title is conveyed by means of a general warranty deed which means that the seller is representing that he has good title and that he is giving clear title to the buyer with the only exceptions being

anything that may be noted in the title insurance policy that the buyer has obtained. Typically a buyer must obtain a title insurance policy for the protection of the lender and may also purchase an owner's title insurance policy for his or her own benefit. Title insurance is designed to insure that any defects in title will be cleared by the title insurance company or the title insurance company will have to pay the buyer or lender for any costs incurred as a result of problems with the title.

6. <u>Closing cost and taxes</u>: The contract should set forth various closing costs that may be associated with the transaction. Typically any real estate property taxes would be the responsibility of the person who holds title up to the date of closing and thereafter will be the responsibility of the purchaser. In some instances there may be what is known as roll back taxes which could come into play once the property is sold. The contract needs to address who is responsible for those.

7. <u>Personal property, fixtures or equipment</u>: If there is any personal property, mechanical equipment or other fixtures or furniture that are being conveyed as part of the transaction then the contract should indicate that all of those items will be conveyed in the same condition that they were in as of the date of the contract being signed.

8. <u>Ratification</u>: The contract should expressly indicate what the date of ratification is. The date of ratification is the date wherein all offers, counter offers, and counter demands have either been accepted or rejected. The date of ratification is the date upon which the parties have come to a complete agreement on all of the issues addressed in the written contract. That date of ratification is important because any contingency periods or other dates set forth in the contract will flow from that date of ratification. As such there should be a statement at the end of the contract expressly indicating the date of ratification.

9. <u>Representations of seller and buyer</u>: If there are any

representations being made either by the seller or the buyer then those should be set forth in the contract. Typical representations made by the seller are that he has good title, that there are no pending suits or actions that might impede or adversely affect the sale of the property, that there is no pending bankruptcy, that sale of the property will not result in any breach or default on his part and that there are no hazardous substances on the property. Typical representations by the purchaser is that if the purchaser is a corporation or partnership that he has full authority to purchase the property and to sign the contract.

10. <u>Risk of loss</u>: This is an important provision in any contract dealing with real estate that has any structures on it. Once a contract has been ratified for the sale of real estate the risk of loss may shift to the buyer. That is, if the structure on that piece of real estate burns down then it is the buyer's loss at that time even though he has not actually gone to settlement on the piece of property. Therefore it is important that the contract expressly state the risk of loss does not pass to the buyer until the date of closing.

11. <u>Real estate commissions</u>: If there are any real estate agents involved it must be expressly stated what their commission is. If there are no real estate agents involved then that likewise should be expressly stated.

12. <u>Attorney fees</u>: Payment of attorney's fees should be addressed in the event there is a breach or default by either party. That is, if litigation results, then it should be stated whether the prevailing party would be entitled to his attorney's fees.

I. **<u>BUSINESS ORGANIZATION</u>**

A business may be conducted in a number of a different forms. Those forms consist of a sole proprietorship, a partnership, a limited partnership, a corporation or a limited liability company.

A sole proprietorship is simply a business that is owned by a single individual. If I operate my business simply in the name of Brien A. Roche, Attorney at Law, then that is a sole proprietorship. A sole proprietorship is an individual conducting business in his own name. That sole proprietorship may have employees and may have several different business locations, but the entire business is owned by a single individual.

A partnership on the other hand is a joint venture of two or more people wherein there is a sharing of both profits and losses. Partnerships can come in different forms. The two most common forms are general partnerships and limited partnerships. A general partnership is where all of the partners share in profits and liabilities of the partnership. That does not necessarily mean that the sharing is equal. The sharing of profits and liabilities may be governed by the partnership agreement that the parties have entered into. A limited partnership on the other hand is a legal entity wherein there typically is only one general partner and there may be a number of limited partners. Those limited partners are much like investors or stockholders in a corporation. The limited partners normally have no control over the operation of the partnership. They have simply contributed funds as an investment in the partnership and then expect to receive some return on their investment when the partnership begins to make money. Typically the sole rights of a limited partner are to share in the profits according to their partnership agreement.

A corporation is a legal entity recognized by state law and created under state law. A corporation can be formed by one or more individuals. The principal benefits of a corporation are to shield the individual conducting the business from personal liability for their contract obligations and to provide for the perpetual existence of the business. If the ABC Corporation enters into a lease with a landlord and then the ABC Corporation defaults on that lease, the landlord's claim for breach of the lease is against the ABC Corporation and not against the individuals who own the corporation. The shield from liability, however, only applies to contract claims and not to tort claims. For instance, if I am the owner of the ABC Corporation and while driving a company vehicle, I run a red light and injure someone then I may be sued along with my company known as the ABC Corporation. If one of my employees, however, is operating a company vehicle, runs a red light and injures someone, then the parties who potentially may be liable as a result of that traffic accident are the employee who was driving and the ABC Corporation. I, as the owner of the ABC Corporation, would not be personably liable. There are instances where corporate officers, directors and controlling shareholders can be liable for tort actions of the corporation if in fact they have implemented a policy that is deemed to be negligent. For instance, if I am the president of a large delivery company and I have implemented a policy requiring that all packages be delivered to the recipient within thirty minutes of receipt by the delivery company then at least under the law of some states, I could be personally liable for that policy because I should know that policy is going to induce my drivers to drive at a high rate of speed and probably in a reckless manner thereby causing automobile accidents.

A corporation is formed by filing the appropriate documents with the state agency that supervises corporations. That document typically would contain the name of the corporation, who the initial directors are, what the purpose of the corporation is and the name and address of the registered agent who has been appointed by the corporation for the purpose of receiving important papers or legal documents. I had mentioned above that one of the benefits of a corporation is to shield the incorporators from personal liability. A second benefit of a corporation is that a corporation has perpetual existence. That is, the corporation does not die when the president dies but rather it continues to exist until it is terminated under the terms of state law.

Once a corporate charter has been issued by the state agency, then it is necessary to have an organizational meeting of the corporation wherein a board of directors is elected, officers are elected, bylaws approved and typically at that time shares of stock are issued. Corporations may be privately held (privately held corporations are frequently referred to as close corporations) or it may be publicly held. A corporation that is publicly held is one that is offering its shares of stock for purchase by members of the public. Many publicly traded corporations are on the various stock exchanges consisting of the New York Stock Exchange, the Nasdaq Exchange and the American Stock Exchange. Not every publicly held corporation is listed on one of those stock exchanges.

As part of the organization of a corporation, bylaws are enacted by the board of directors. Bylaws are the constitution of the corporation that set forth the basic framework as to how the corporation will be operated. In addition, the shareholders may enter into a shareholder's agreement. A shareholder's agreement is a contract entered into between the shareholders in a privately held corporation that will govern their conduct in the event of the three D's: death, disability or deadlock. That is, the shareholder's agreement will govern what will happen in the event that one of the shareholders dies, becomes disabled or in the event that there is a deadlock between the shareholders as to how the corporation is to be conducted. The shareholder's agreement may also govern a number of other rights between the shareholders.

After a corporation has been duly formed, there may be periodic reporting requirements to the state where the corporation has been formed. Those reporting requirements call for the corporation to report its current address, the name and address of its registered agent and the name and address of its directors and officers.

A corporation may be terminated by filing a notice or articles of termination or dissolution with the appropriate state agency. The mere fact that articles of termination or dissolution have been filed with the state agency does not mean that the debts of that corporation evaporate. If in fact the persons who control the corporation have raided the corporation and stripped it of its assets and thereby defrauded its creditors, then those individuals who are the owners may become personally liable for that fraudulent behavior.

Other forms of business organization are limited liability companies and limited liability partnerships. A limited liability company is very similar to a corporation but the reporting requirements to the state agency are generally less strenuous. A limited liability partnership is a partnership wherein the partners are allowed to limit their particular liability for the conduct of other partners. One of the oddities of partnership law is that each partner is liable for the conduct or misconduct of all other partners in the course of performing their partnership duties. Through a limited liability partnership the partners can limit their liability.

J. **BANKRUPTCY**

Bankruptcy law is a body of federal law that is contained in the United States Code. This body of law has supplanted or replaced any state law, whether it be statutory or case law, dealing with issues of bankruptcy. The U.S. Congress years ago felt that the issue of bankruptcy was sufficiently important that it needed to codify the law and thereby supplant any state laws that may exist in regards to bankruptcy.

The general thrust of our bankruptcy laws is to provide protection to individuals or businesses who are in financial distress in order to either eventually give them a discharge from those financial obligations or in other instances to give them some breathing room so as to be able to deal with their financial difficulties, hopefully get back on their feet and then be able to repay their obligations either in whole or in part.

One of the main purposes of bankruptcy is to relieve an honest debtor of debts, thereby providing an opportunity for a fresh start. The bankruptcy laws also benefit creditors by providing a forum for either an orderly disposition of whatever assets a debtor may have or a plan for full or partial repayment of creditors. Creditors may be either secured or unsecured. A secured creditor may generally be thought of as someone that has a security interest or what might be referred to as a lien interest or mortgage against a piece of property. An unsecured creditor is someone like a credit card company or the telephone company that has no security to rely on.

In each federal district the Bankruptcy Court constitutes a unit of that U.S. District Court and receives its authority to hear cases and proceedings by referral from that U.S. District Court.

Bankruptcy Court Judges are appointed by the U.S. Courts of Appeals for that particular circuit to fourteen year terms.

The three basic types of bankruptcy filings are referred to as chapter seven proceedings, chapter eleven proceedings and chapter thirteen proceedings.

Some basic principles that apply to all bankruptcy proceedings are the following:

1. The debtor (the person filing the bankruptcy) is required by law to list all of his assets. If there is any hiding of assets, then that may subject the debtor to criminal prosecution.
2. The debtor must list all of his debts. Any debts that are not listed will not be discharged.
3. Any debts incurred within ninety days prior to the bankruptcy filing are generally deemed not to be dischargeable. That is, you cannot go out and run up ten thousand dollars of credit card debt and then run into bankruptcy the next day. If you do, then the ten thousand dollars of credit card debt may not be discharged in the bankruptcy proceeding.
4. Upon the filing of a bankruptcy petition there is an automatic stay that is entered by the court that precludes creditors (persons who claim that the debtor owes them money) from filing any sort of civil action against the debtor. That automatic stay continues until the court lifts the stay or until there is a discharge granted to the debtor.
5. After filing for bankruptcy there will be a creditor's hearing at which time the creditors may appear and examine the debtor as to the location and extent of his assets and the validity of any other debts that are claimed.
6. Those persons who are making a claim against the debtor are required to file a proof of claim. Those claims will then be given certain priority. The claims that have the highest priority are the ones that are most likely to be paid in full. Other claims that

have lower priority may only be partially paid or may not be paid at all.
7. An individual debtor is entitled to certain exemptions either under the bankruptcy code or pursuant to applicable state law. These exemptions allow the debtor to essentially keep certain things. Those things may consist of such items as a motor vehicle, certain household goods, books and papers and other things that may assist in the production of income.
8. The objective in most instances of a bankruptcy filing is either to gain some breathing room from the attempts by creditors to collect against the debtor or ultimately to receive a discharge. There are some debts, however, that are not dischargeable. Certain debts such as taxes, alimony and child support, certain student loans and several other categories of debts may not be dischargeable. Once a discharge has been entered then the debtor is relieved of all personal liability for those discharged debts. A discharge automatically voids any judgment against the debtor for personal liability on a debt and acts as a permanent injunction prohibiting creditors from acting to recover the discharged debt from that debtor personally. The debtor may, however, reaffirm the debt if he wishes. That reaffirmation must meet specific requirements in order to be valid.

A chapter seven proceeding is one filed by an individual, partnership or corporation wherein they have to disclose all of their debts to the court and then disclose what assets they have if any to satisfy those liabilities. If they have no assets to satisfy the debts then they will eventually be granted a discharge and their debts are wiped out. If they do have assets to satisfy the debts, then the court may order a distribution of those assets in order to satisfy the debts before granting a discharge. A discharge under chapter seven may only be granted to an individual person. That is a partnership or corporation cannot receive a discharge.

A second form of bankruptcy is known as a chapter eleven filing. A chapter eleven filing is generally referred to as a business reorganization and may be filed either by an individual or by a corporation. The general purpose of a chapter eleven filing is to allow the business or individual some breathing room from the onslaught of its creditors so as to allow the business/individual to get back on its feet and then hopefully repay the creditors in whole or in part. This type of bankruptcy may involve the appointment of a bankruptcy trustee who is a court official who supervises the progress of the bankruptcy case. In some chapter eleven proceedings all of the assets of the debtor may be transferred to the trustee which means that the debtor cannot convey any assets without approval of that trustee. The trustee may actually take over running the business of the debtor. In other cases the debtor may remain in possession of all assets. The objective of a chapter eleven filing is to submit to the court a plan of reorganization or rehabilitation setting forth a method by which the debts and obligations of the debtor may be paid off so as to allow the business to continue. If that plan is never accepted by the court, then the bankruptcy filing will be dismissed. If the plan is accepted by the court, then the debtor is expected to comply with that plan over the period of time allowed. If in fact the plan is complied with by the debtor, then the debtor will eventually come out of bankruptcy and lose the protection of the bankruptcy court. Upon confirmation of the plan, those plans provisions are binding on all creditors and on the debtor. Once the plan has been confirmed by the court then the debtor is discharged from all pre-confirmation debts as well as certain other types of debts. The debtor is required to implement the plan and to comply with all court orders. The Court of course has the authority to enforce its orders. Some chapter eleven cases may progress as liquidation proceedings; i.e., debtor may maintain possession of all of his assets for the purpose of gathering them together and then liquidating or selling them. This is sometimes allowed if it appears that the debtor can get more money for these assets than could the trustee in bankruptcy.

A third form of bankruptcy filing is a chapter thirteen filing known as a wage earners plan. This type of bankruptcy can only be filed by people who receive regular wages as their form of compensation. For instance, a person who works at the phone company and receives a pay check every two weeks could file a wage earner's plan. A medical doctor, however, who works for himself and receives compensation simply in the form of profits from his business could not file a wage earners plan. There are also limitations on the amount of debt a person may have to file under this chapter. Under chapter thirteen a discharge is granted to the debtor once he has made all payments under the plan unless that has been waived.

In summary chapter seven (7) cases may be thought of as <u>liquidation</u> proceedings where the assets (if any) are liquidated (converted to cash) and used to satisfy creditors in the order of priority established. A chapter eleven case is generally a <u>business reorganization</u> proceeding where the debtor expects to continue operating. A wage earner's proceeding under chapter 13 is designed to provide payment to creditors with the wage earner receiving an eventual discharge.

K. **EMPLOYMENT**

The employment relationship between employer and employee is essentially a contractual relationship. That is if I offer you a job with my company and you accept that offer then we have entered into a contract. All of the elements of a contract have been satisfied in that there has been an offer made, acceptance of the offer by you with the consideration being the wages that you will be paid in return for your services. Sometimes people enter into written contracts of employment. If there is a written contract of employment then that contract is to be reviewed and analyzed the same as any other contract. If there is a breach of that contract by either party then there may be a resulting claim or lawsuit made for that breach of contract.

More often than not contracts of employment are purely oral.

If I advertise a position available in the local newspaper, you respond to that advertisement, I interview you and then offer you employment which you then accept, then there has been a contract of employment entered into with most of the terms of that contract being oral. The advertisement that ran in the newspaper was in written form and that writing (advertisement) would be written evidence of what the terms of the contract are; however, other terms of the contract probably would be oral. That oral contract of employment is every bit as valid as a written contract of employment. One caveat or restriction on that would be any limitation that may be imposed by the statute of frauds that may exist in that state where the employment is based. The statute of frauds is statutory law that can vary from state to state that may require that certain types of contracts be in writing to be enforceable. Contracts that cannot be performed within one year are frequently governed by the statute of frauds. If I offered you employment for five years, and that offer and your acceptance were purely oral, then that contract may not be enforceable for that five year period because obviously a five year employment contract cannot be performed in one year and therefore would not be enforceable for its full term in light of the statute of frauds.

Even though a contract of employment may be in writing there may be other evidence as to what the terms of that contract of employment are aside from any advertisements for employment and any oral agreements that may have been entered into. If the employer has an employee manual then that employee manual may set forth basic terms of employment that could be evidence as to what the actual contract terms are. Likewise if there were any subsequent written statements made by the employer or statements in writing agreed to between the employer and the employee relating to the employment status then all of that may be evidence as to what the terms of the contract are.

Although the foundation stone of the employment relationship is the contract, oral or written, the employment relationship is also governed by federal, state and local statutes and ordinances. At the federal level there are several statutes that have been passed by Congress that prohibit discrimination by employers. Similar statutes may exist at the state level and also at the local level. Discrimination based upon race, sex, religion, national origin, sexual preference and marital status may all be addressed in these different statutes and ordinances. At the federal level there are several different statutes dealing with employment discrimination. Title VII of the Civil Rights Act of 1964 contained in 42 USC §2000(e) prohibits discrimination in employment including hiring, firing, compensation, terms, conditions or privileges of employment on the basis of race, color, religion, sex or national origin. This federal statute like many federal statutes only applies to employers that have a certain number of employees. The logic behind this requirement goes to some of the constitutional issues that we had talked about in regards to the limited authority of the federal government. The federal government being a government of limited authority or jurisdiction cannot simply pass laws that govern every aspect of our lives without there being some constitutional basis for that law. The federal government is able to invoke that constitutional basis in regards to much of its legislation because of the impact that certain things may have upon interstate commerce. A small employer with only one employee probably has no real impact on interstate commerce. However, an employer with fifteen employees probably does have some impact, although it may be remote, on interstate commerce and therefore such employers may be governed by this federal statute. Section 1981 of the Civil Rights Act of 1866 found in 42 USC §1981 prohibits race discrimination in employment. Section 1983 of the Civil Rights Act of 1871 found in 42 USC §1983 prohibits discrimination on the basis of race under color of state law. What that means is that there must be a state agency or employee involved in the discriminatory act. The Age Discrimination in Employment Act found in 29 USC §621 covers employers with twenty or more employees and sets up a protected age group between ages forty and seventy with certain exceptions. The Equal Pay Act found in 29 USC §206(d) deals with discrimination in wages on the basis of sex. Title IX of the Education Amendments of 1972 found at 20 USC §1682 prohibits discrimination in employment.

Claims under Title VII referenced above can be brought on a theory of disparate treatment or disparate impact. Disparate treatment generally involves some intentional discrimination or it can be founded upon the fact that similarly situated persons of different races receive different treatment without an adequate non-racial explanation. A disparate impact claim on the other hand rather than looking at the specific treatment of individuals looks at the impact that it has. That is, the particular employment practice at issue may be on its face neutral but the result that it has upon a particular racial group may be more harsh on that group than it is on other groups. That may be a basis for a discrimination claim. Another federal statute that may have an impact on employment is the Americans With Disability Act found at 42 USC §12101 which prohibits employers from discriminating against qualified individuals with a disability with respect to all aspects of employment including job application procedures, hiring, advancement or discharge. The general intent of this statute is to require employers to make some reasonable accommodations for disabled persons so as to assure that they are treated on an equal footing with other qualified individuals. In 1993 the Congress passed the Family and Medical Leave Act. This federal statute permits employees to take up to ninety days of paid or unpaid leave for family medical emergencies. This applies to all public sector employers and private employers with fifty or more workers. Some state have passed statutes of a similar nature.

Employment discrimination claims over the years have not only involved discrimination against minority groups but also so called reverse discrimination claims wherein white plaintiffs claim that they are discriminated against because of favored treatment given to minority groups. Likewise a discrimination claim may involve a claim of retaliation wherein an employee states that he has filed a discrimination complaint and there is retaliation by the employer. Retaliation is dealt with separately under these federal statutes. In regards to any of these discrimination claims brought under federal law it is important to keep in mind that they may have very specific requirements that have to be met as far as filing your claim, how your claim is to be filed and then when suit can be filed. Typically the charge of discrimination has to be brought within a fairly short period of time after the discriminatory conduct has been engaged in by the employer. You must bring that claim to the appropriate administrative agency which then has the opportunity to investigate it and then you must either await the conclusion at that administrative level or otherwise await the passage of a certain amount of time before you can actually file suit against the employer. All of those requirements are very specific and dictated by the statute that you are suing under. Similar types of requirements may be called for in regards to any claims brought under state statutory provisions or local ordinances. The general framework of these statutes is to require that the employee bring the claim promptly so that the employer is given prompt notice of the charge made by the employee so that the employer then has the opportunity to investigate the claim and likewise the appropriate federal or state agency can investigate the claim. If that investigation does not resolve the matter then the employee will eventually acquire the right to file a civil action against the employer.

In many states, in the absence of an express contract for employment, an employee is considered to be an employee at will. An employee at will is free to leave that employment at any time the employee wishes and likewise the employer is free to terminate the employment any time he wishes. When the employee is considered to be an employee at will then the only restriction imposed upon the employer is simply that he cannot terminate the employment for a discriminatory reason in violation of one of the federal statutes referenced above or state or local statutes that may apply and likewise may not terminate the employment for a reason that would violate what is referred to as public policy. For instance, if an employee in the course of his employment discovers that the employer is defrauding the federal government with whom he has a contract and the employee complains of that and thereafter is terminated for that reason then even though the employment relationship in that context may have been "at will" the employee may still have a basis for a wrongful discharge claim against the employer.

Unemployment compensation laws are an aspect of employment law. Unemployment compensation is a state and federal funding system to provide compensation to people who are unemployed for a period of time.

If you are laid off from your position, then you may be entitled to unemployment compensation benefits for a certain period time. Those benefits do not go on forever. The expectation is that eventually you will find new work and therefore the benefits do have a termination date to them.

Your entitlement to unemployment compensation benefits may differ from state to state. In general, however, you are entitled to unemployment compensation benefits unless you voluntarily left your employment or unless you were dismissed from the employment due to some misconduct on your part. The misconduct typically must be fairly serious in order to defeat your claim for unemployment compensation benefits.

L. **WORKER'S COMPENSATION**

Workers compensation is a form of insurance coverage that is designed to protect the working person in the event of injury.

In a worker's compensation claim the parties involved are the injured worker, his employer and the employer's worker's compensation insurance company. Before the passage of worker's compensation laws a worker who was injured on the job was forced to file suit against his employer and potentially wait for months or even years before he ever received any compensation for that injury. That produced a result wherein the worker and his family may have no income for an extended period of time because the worker was injured and unable to work and further the worker was unable to pay for medical treatment. If the worker did eventually recover from the employer in a civil action, then that award of money damages frequently came too late for the worker since at that point he was destitute and perhaps permanently impaired because of the lack of proper medical treatment.

As such, many states nearly one hundred years ago began

passing worker's compensation laws which provided a type of compromise. That is, the worker upon being injured did not have to prove any fault on the part of the employer but simply had to prove that he was on the job and that the injury arose out of his employment. If he could prove those two things then he was entitled to receive a portion of his wages for that period of time when he was disabled and further was entitled to appropriate medical treatment related to that injury. In return for that, the employer received immunity from a civil claim brought by the employee for the injury. That is, the employee could not file a civil action against the employer. The employee's exclusive remedy is the worker's compensation benefits referenced above.

Every state has its own worker's compensation law and that law can vary dramatically from state to state. The general thrust, however, of the worker's compensation system nationwide is as stated above. In addition, there are worker's compensation acts that operate at the federal level. Individuals employed by the federal government are covered by the Federal Employees Compensation Act which is a worker's compensation act that is administered by the U.S. Department of Labor. There is also another federal statute known as the Longshoremen and Harbor Worker's Act which is an act that technically covers longshoreman and harbor workers but also covers private employees who are working on defense installations who are not federal employees and also covers private employees who are working overseas who are covered by the Defense Base Act which is a type of worker's compensation act that incorporates the Longshoremen and Harbor Workers Act.

Worker's compensation acts around the country are administered by a governmental agency for that jurisdiction which administers claims filed by workers. If an employee is injured on the job, then he must report that injury to his employer within a designated period of time and file a written report of that injury. If in fact he is forced to lose time from work or requires medical treatment, then he may file a claim with the administrative agency that administers worker's compensation claims for that jurisdiction. Once a claim is filed, then the employer can either contest or accept the claim. If the employer accepts the claim, then that means that the employer is agreeing that the employee was injured on the job and that the injury arose out of the employment and that the employee is entitled to medical coverage and perhaps to wage benefits for the time that he is disabled. If the employer decides to challenge the claim, then there will be a hearing before an administrative law judge or a hearing officer who will then make a decision as to whether the claim is compensable and whether the employee should be paid wage benefits and/or medical benefits.

There has been a good bit of litigation over the years as to exactly what constitutes being an employee. Typically a person who is an independent contractor will not qualify as an employee under the worker's compensation act. Likewise, the individual who is the owner of the business may not qualify as an employee unless he has expressly chosen to include himself in that definition within the policy of insurance issued.

Wage benefits are calculated based upon what is referred to as the average weekly wage. That is, the wages of the employee over a period of time are totaled up and then averaged. Once that average has been calculated, then the employee is typically entitled to two thirds of that average weekly wage (up to a statutory ceiling).

The second principle form of benefit received under worker's compensation is that of medical coverage. That is, if an employee is injured on the job then he is entitled to reasonable and necessary hospital and medical treatment related to that injury to hopefully get him back on his feet and able to resume his employment. If he is not able to resume his former employment, then he may be entitled to rehabilitation services that will either allow him to return to some other form of employment or be trained in a new line of work.

If an employee is injured on the job as a result of the fault of some third person, then that employee may have a basis for a claim (sometimes referred to as a third party claim) against that other individual or company. For instance, suppose you are working on a construction job and you are employed by the general contractor. If while performing those duties, an employee of a plumbing sub-contractor drops a pipe that strikes you on the head then you may be entitled to the benefits called for under the Act. In addition to being compensated under The Worker's Compensation Act, you may also have a basis for a claim against the plumbing sub-contractor whose employee dropped the pipe on you. In some states, on a construction job such as this, all contractors may be immune from suit by any other employee on that construction job. In other states, the employee may sue any other responsible contractor on the job. If the injured employee in that circumstance does recover money from the third party who caused the injury, then the employer of that injured worker, or more likely the employer's insurance carrier, is entitled to recover all or part of the monies paid to the worker under The Worker's Compensation Act. This is a principle known as subrogation. Subrogation literally means that one party is subrogated or steps into the shoes of another party in terms of acquiring their rights. Under most worker's compensation acts, once the employee makes a claim for benefits and receives benefits, then to the extent that the employee has any right of recovery against a third party, the employer or its insurance carrier is subrogated to or steps into the shoes of that employee and acquires that right of recovery that the employee has against the third party to the extent of the amount of wage and income benefits paid to the employee. The purpose of allowing subrogation in this type of instance is to hold down the cost of worker's compensation insurance coverage and further to prevent the employee from receiving a double recovery on the wages and medical benefits received. If the employee is compensated under The Worker's Compensation Act and then further compensated for the same injuries as a result of the third party civil claim, that to some extent constitutes a double recovery to the employee. After paying back amounts paid to him for wage and medical benefits under the Worker's Compensation Act, the employee is entitled to keep any excess award by a jury or received in settlement.

The law relating to worker's compensation coverage can become extremely complex when dealing with issues of occupational disease. The run of the mill on the job injury where an employee falls and breaks his ankle does not involve a great deal of controversy. However, the claim of the employee who over a period of time develops carpel tunnel syndrome as a result of typing at the keyboard becomes a bit more problematic as to whether that truly was a result of the employment. Different states have dealt with that issue in a variety of ways. Some states provide coverage for these types of repetitive stress injuries or exposure injuries; other states do not provide coverage. Another area of significant controversy in regards to worker's compensation claims is that of compensation for emotional injuries. That is, the employee who suffers a nervous breakdown because of emotional stress on the job under some worker's compensation acts may be entitled to the whole range of benefits under the workers compensation system. Other states have denied those types of benefits on the theory that the relationship between the employment and the emotional injury is simply too tenuous and therefore the employer should not be made to bear the burden of the expense associated with that type of injury.

A final type of compensation that the employee may be entitled to as a result of an on the job injury is compensation for permanent disability. Most workers compensation acts have created a schedule wherein specific disabilities are worth a certain amount of weeks of wages. For instance, a person who loses a foot may be entitled to one hundred and fifty weeks of wages over and above any other wages that he may have received. A person who loses an eye on the job may be entitled to an equivalent amount of compensation. Those forms of compensation are over and above the wage loss benefits otherwise paid and any medical expenses that have been paid.

Worker's compensation claims can be complicated in instances where an individual has suffered an injury while employed with one company and then goes to work for another company and a year later re-injures himself. Which employer is going to be responsible for that compensation? Some states have set up what is referred to as a second injury fund wherein that second injury while in the course of the employment of the second company will be partially paid out of that second injury fund and then also partially paid by the second company. That second injury fund is a fund of money that is created by contributions from all of the different insurance companies that underwrite worker's compensation insurance coverage in that jurisdiction.

A similar type of fund that may exist is the uninsured employer's fund. An employer who has not taken out worker's compensation coverage and who therefore cannot pay the benefits called for under the worker's compensation act may still be covered in the sense the employee may make a claim against the uninsured employer's fund. To the extent that any payments are made out of that fund, then typically the fund or the attorney general of that state will make a claim against the uninsured employer in order to recover such payments.

In the event that an employee is killed on the job, then the family of that employee who is financially dependent upon the employee is entitled to death benefits. Those death benefits are wage benefits that will at least in part replace the loss of income as a result of the death of the employee.

There has been a good deal of controversy over the extent to which worker's compensation laws should provide benefits to injured employees. Many states put a cap on the amount of wage benefits that the employee can receive. That is, in some jurisdictions the employee can receive no more than five hundred weeks of wage benefits which is the equivalent of approximately ten years of benefits. This is to the advantage of the employer in that it puts a limitation on what the employer's or the insurer's liability is. Obviously it may be a detriment to the employee if the employee is in fact permanently disabled and cannot return to any form of work. If in fact the employee is permanently and totally disabled, then he may be able to extend those benefits under state law; however, proving that a worker is both permanently and totally disabled is not an easy task. As such, in many states employees are left in a situation where they cannot return to their former employment yet at the end of ten years their wage benefits are terminated.

There also is a good bit of controversy in regards to the provision of medical treatment to injured workers. Typically the medical treatment is controlled by the employer or the employer's insurance carrier which means that the employee is receiving treatment from doctors who have been chosen by the insurance carrier or the employer. These doctors obviously know who is paying their bill and they know that the insurance carrier and the employer expect this employee to return to work at some point in time so that their financial exposure in terms of paying wage benefits is limited. Although these doctors generally provide quality medical care for the injured employee, they obviously have a somewhat mixed loyalty in that they know that the employer and the insurance company want this employee to return to work whereas the employee and the doctor may know that it is not necessarily always in the employee's interest to return to work too quickly or even to return to that form of work at all. These are issues that are becoming more commonly addressed with the advent of managed care health insurance policies.

M. **INSURANCE**

An insurance policy is a contract. The parties to the contract are the insurance company and the insured (you). In addition there may sometimes be a beneficiary or what may be referred to as a third party beneficiary of an insurance contract. In a life insurance policy, the beneficiary is the person who receives the death benefits upon the death of the person who was insured. In an automobile insurance policy, the third party beneficiary under a liability policy is the individual who was injured and who receives compensation from that liability insurance policy. The beneficiary or third party beneficiary is not a named party to the insurance contract but is generally the person who is intended to benefit from the insurance policy. As such that beneficiary may have certain rights under the policy.

There are a variety of different types of insurance policies that can be written. The most common types of policies are liability, life insurance and health insurance policies.

The type of insurance coverage that you are probably most familiar with is that of automobile insurance coverage. An automobile policy may include several different forms of coverage. That is, within one policy there may be liability coverage, there may be medical expense coverage, there may be collision coverage and there may be uninsured/underinsured motorist coverage. Each of those different types of coverage are dramatically different and each of them has a different objective. Liability coverage is designed to protect you, the insured, in the event you are involved in a collision wherein some other person is injured as a result of your supposed negligence. If in fact a person is injured and they contend that you are negligent then they may assert a liability claim against you alleging that you owe them for their medical expenses, lost wages, pain and suffering, resulting disabilities, disfigurement, etc. Your liability insurance policy would cover you in that instance by providing you with an attorney to defend you in that claim and further indemnifying you for any judgment rendered against you in that case up to your policy limits. If your policy limits are fifty thousand dollars and the claim that is made against you under the liability policy is worth five hundred thousand dollars and there is a judgment entered against you for that five hundred thousand dollars, then your insurance company is only obliged to pay fifty thousand dollars and the remaining four hundred and fifty thousand dollars may well come out of your pocket.

Also within a automobile insurance policy there may be comprehensive coverage. Comprehensive coverage is what is referred to as a type of first party coverage wherein you may make a claim against your own policy as a result of damage to your vehicle. If your vehicle was damaged in a collision and you do not wish to or cannot assert a claim against the other party that you contend may have been at fault, or if you were at fault, then you may make a claim against your own policy under your collision coverage. Your insurance company will then pay you for the repair cost of your vehicle. In the event your vehicle is totaled it will then pay you the fair market value for that vehicle. If someone other than you was at fault, your insurance company may then have a right of recovery against that other driver. Most forms of collision coverage do carry a deductible which means that you would only be compensated by your insurance carrier for that amount of money that exceeded your deductible amount.

Auto insurance coverage also offers what is referred to as medical expense coverage or personal injury protection coverage. Medical expense coverage is again a type of first party coverage wherein you may make a claim against your own insurance company for medical expenses incurred as a result of a collision If you are injured in an automobile collision while in your car you can make a claim against your policy for payment of your medical expenses to the extent that they were reasonable and necessary as a result of this collision. If you are a passenger in someone else's vehicle then, assuming there is medical payments coverage for the vehicle you are riding in, you can also make a claim for medical payments under that policy. You may be able to make a claim for medical payments under both your policy and the policy of the vehicle you are riding in.

Another form of coverage under a typical automobile insurance policy is known as uninsured or underinsured motorist coverage. This is a very important form of coverage because it protects you in the event that you are involved in a collision that is the fault of an uninsured or underinsured motorist. Suppose you are hit from the rear by a vehicle that is uninsured and you are injured. You of course could make a claim against the driver of that striking vehicle but, if that driver is uninsured, then whatever claim you make against that driver may be all for naught because he has no insurance coverage and may have no assets to pay any judgment that you may obtain against him. In that instance, your own uninsured motorist coverage would apply in which event your insurance company could essentially step in and defend that uninsured motorist or at least take a position that is contrary to you in terms of challenging your claims for uninsured motorist benefits. The same basic principle would apply if that striking vehicle was underinsured. Suppose the vehicle that struck you from behind had twenty five thousand dollars in coverage but your medical expenses as a result of the collision are fifty thousand dollars. The striking motorist would then be underinsured. If you made a claim against him for one hundred and fifty thousand dollars including the fifty thousand medical expenses, an income loss claim, pain and suffering and you got a judgment for that amount, would he be able to pay it? He probably would not be able to pay it. His insurance policy would pay the first twenty five thousand dollars and anything over and above that would be covered by your policy to the extent that you had underinsured motorist coverage. Uninsured motorist coverage is a very broad form of coverage. Suppose you are a bicyclist or even a pedestrian, and you are struck by an uninsured motorist or by a hit and run motorist. In that circumstance you may make a claim for and recover under your own uninsured motorist coverage even though you were not in a vehicle at the time.

Another form of insurance is life insurance coverage. A life insurance policy is simply a contract between you, the insured, and the insurance company wherein the insurance company agrees to pay a certain amount of benefits upon your death. Assuming that there have been no misrepresentations made by you in terms of applying for this type of insurance coverage, then your survivors simply make a claim to that insurance company upon your passing and the designated beneficiary will then receive the benefits due. There are different types of life insurance coverage. The most common form of life insurance coverage these days is term life insurance. Term life insurance policies have no value other than the face amount of the policy and even then have no value unless the person who is insured passes away during the coverage period. Another type of life insurance coverage is that of whole life coverage which actually is a type of investment wherein the value of the policy may increase over a period of time as you pay premiums and further may allow you to take loans against the policy and perhaps even redeem the policy for a fixed amount of money. The theory behind whole life or universal life is that you not only are insuring your life but you are also making an investment that is increasing in value over a period of time which you may utilize in the form of taking a loan against it or in terms of cashing it in. In our current economic environment, whole life insurance policies probably are not good investments since the rate of return is generally fairly low.

Another type of insurance coverage is health insurance

coverage. Health insurance contracts are frequently group insurance contracts wherein you as a member of a group pay a premium to the insurance company in return for the insurance company agreeing to cover medical and hospital expenses up to certain limits. The general limitation in terms of the scope of coverage under these policies is that the treatment that you receive must be reasonable and necessary and the cost of the treatment must be consistent with the usual and customary charges for other practitioners in the area. For instance, if you decide to have plastic surgery that is purely elective, this type of treatment may not be covered unless you have a special endorsement or provision within your policy that provides coverage since the treatment is not necessary. Likewise, if you choose to go to the most expensive orthopaedic surgeon in the area because you think he is the best, then all of the charges rendered by that surgeon may not be covered under your policy because the policy is governed by what is usual and customary for those types of services and not necessarily by what the best practitioner in that area may charge.

Another type of insurance coverage is homeowner's insurance coverage. A homeowner's policy typically includes a fire endorsement which would cover you in the event that your house, including contents, burns down. It is important in reviewing that type of coverage that you make sure that the stated value is in fact consistent with the replacement cost or the fair market value of the house. For instance, if you are in a geographical area where property values are increasing dramatically, then it is important that you likewise increase the covered amount under this provision of your homeowner's policy so as to make sure that there is enough money paid to you in the event that your house does burn down. Likewise, within this type of policy there may be coverage for water damage, theft, and also for liability claims. Liability may arise in a homeowner's context where a guest is on your premises and the guest is injured as a result of some defect on the premises. For instance, suppose there is a large hole in your back yard that is covered by overgrown grass and your guest falls into that hole and breaks his ankle. Is the guest going to be able to make a liability claim against you? They probably will because arguably there is some negligence on your part in that you did not disclose to the guest that the hole was in your backyard even though you knew the guest was out there walking around. In that type of circumstance, the guest may make a liability claim against you alleging that there is negligence on your part and if in fact a judge or jury were to agree with that then the liability insurance policy would have to indemnify you up to your policy limits. Under this type of liability policy, the liability insurance carrier would also provide an attorney to defend you.

We had previously talked about liability insurance policies. Most of the litigation relating to insurance issues involves liability insurance policies: automobile, homeowners or professional liability. We have already discussed automobile and homeowners liability coverage. If you were a medical doctor you most likely would have a malpractice insurance policy covering you. That malpractice insurance policy is a form of liability coverage that would apply in an instance where a patient sues you for malpractice. In that event, the malpractice insurance company would step in, conduct an investigation and determine if the claim should be adjusted or negotiated. In the event the insurance company does not settle your patient's claim, the patient may file suit against you in which event the insurance company would appoint an attorney to represent you and then would indemnify you as to any judgment up to the amount of your policy limits.

N. **EMINENT DOMAIN**

You may recall in our review of constitutional law that, if the government takes someone's property for a governmental purpose, then the government must compensate that property owner fairly. The right of the government to take property is known as the right of eminent domain. The government, in fact, does have the right to take property for a public purpose. The mere fact that the government has chosen to take your property does not mean that you as a property owner have to stand by idly. Governmental takings may be challenged on the grounds of necessity. For instance, there has been a fair amount of litigation over the last several years challenging certain governmental takings that were not necessarily motivated by public need but were more motivated by the interest of that governmental authority in acquiring a piece of property and then reselling it for a profit in order in essence to generate income for that governmental entity. That is not an appropriate governmental taking of property. The general rule is that there has to be some need for the property. If there is some bonafide need for a highway then obviously the highway has to go somewhere which means that it is going to go over someone's land. If there happens to be a residential development on that land then it may be that the government has to take that land, compensate the property owners for the loss of their homes and the expense associated with moving and then raze those homes to make way for the highway. The same rationale would apply in regards to acquiring land for parks. Those types of takings are never happy occasions for the government or for the property owners who are affected but the government has to weigh the general public benefit against the particular detriment to a small number of individuals. Obviously if you are one who is on the receiving end of the governmental taking then the overall public need or benefit may not seem to be terribly convincing. Once the government has made a decision to take your property then under the Constitution they are obliged to compensate you fairly for that taking. That compensation is generally based upon a determination as to what the fair market value is of your property. You may feel as if the fair market value is X and the government may feel that the fair market value is one half of X. What do you do in that type of circumstance? Generally, a law suit referred to as an eminent domain action or condemnation action is filed by which the government condemns or takes your property. In bringing this type of action the parties are asking the court to determine what the fair market value is of that property. The actual taking occurs by the government filing at the courthouse what is referred to typically as a Certificate of Take. Upon the filing of that Certificate of Take, the title to that property is transferred to the government. The only issue then to be decided by the court is what the property is worth. That may involve a trial. Different jurisdictions handle these trials in different ways. In some jurisdictions, these types of cases are tried before commissioners. These commissioners may be local citizens or in some instances they are individuals who have been chosen by the court as having some knowledge or expertise in terms of local property values. These commissioners then sit on a jury panel and hear evidence as to what the value of the property is and then make a decision as to what the value is. The evidence they hear is testimony from appraisers and perhaps other property owners as to what this piece of property is worth and what economic effect the taking has upon the property owner.

O. LIENS

A lien is a security interest that one party has in property that is held by another person. For instance, the mortgage against your family home is a lien. The lien holder is the mortgage company to whom you make your monthly payments. The lien itself is the mortgage or what in some jurisdictions may be referred to as the deed of trust which constitutes a security interest against your home. The purpose of that lien or security interest is to secure the mortgage company for the payment of the mortgage. If you fail to make your monthly mortgage payments, then the lien holder; i.e., the mortgage company may foreclose on that lien or mortgage in order to take the property back and then sell it in order to recover the money that they had loaned to you plus their expenses associated with the foreclosure. In the event that you sell the property, your lienholder will be paid in full from the proceeds of the sale.

Liens may also arise in a number of other circumstances. You have probably heard the term "mechanic's lien". Literally, a mechanic's lien is a type of lien that can be filed by a mechanic or material supplier or workman who does work on your real estate. For instance, if you hire a contractor to come into your home and add a bedroom and you do not pay that contractor, then that contractor can file a mechanic's lien at the courthouse.

The purpose of that mechanic's lien is to put the rest of the world on notice of the fact that you owe that contractor an amount of money as set forth in the lien and that the contractor now has a lien or security interest against your property until that debt is paid. If you attempted to sell your property, before any sale could go through, you would have to satisfy that mechanic's lien either by paying it off or by placing an amount of money in escrow to cover it in the event the mechanic's lien was found to be bonafide. Once a mechanic's lien is filed, then typically the mechanic, i.e., the contractor or the material supplier, has a designated amount of time within which to file suit against you to enforce the lien. If suit is not filed within the time allowed then the mechanic's lien is generally considered to be unenforceable although it may not be released of record at the courthouse without further action on your part.

Another type of lien is a garagekeeper's lien. If you store your vehicle in a garage for a period of time and then refuse to pay the garagekeeper, then that garagekeeper may have a lien against your vehicle which may entitle him to hold your vehicle until such time as you pay the obligation that is owed. Likewise if you take your vehicle to a repair shop for repair and then refuse to pay the bill, the repairman may have the right to assert a lien against that vehicle which might entitle him to hold your vehicle until such time as you pay the repair bill. The mere fact that you paid the repair bill does not mean that you cannot then recover that amount by suing the repairman. For instance if the work is not done properly and the repairman attempts to hold your vehicle hostage pending payment of his bill, then you could go ahead and pay the bill in order to get your vehicle back and then sue the repairman in a civil action in order to recover the money that you had paid for the work that was not properly performed.

Another type of lien that may come into existence is an innkeeper's lien. For instance if you go into a motel and spend five nights there and do not pay for the room then the innkeeper may have a lien against whatever personal property you have there on the premises in order to secure the eventual payment of the bill for the room. If you do not pay the bill for the room, then the innkeeper may be entitled to hold that property until the bill is paid.

In terms of domestic relations matters, liens may arise in regards to child support and spousal support. If one spouse does not pay child support or spousal support that is ordered by the court, then by operation of law there may arise a lien against that nonpaying spouse's real estate. That lien will become a matter of public record at the courthouse so that any attempt made by that nonpaying spouse to sell his or her real estate would be potentially blocked by the fact that there was a lien against the real estate for the amount of unpaid child support or spousal support.

Attorneys likewise can acquire liens for their services. For instance if I was hired by you to sue another party who had caused injury to you as a result of their negligence and I performed certain services for you in the course of that representation and then you decide to dismiss me and either retain another attorney or to settle the case on your own, then I may have an attorney's lien against that eventual settlement or judgment amount based upon the reasonable value of my services. Although the fee agreement that may have been in existence between you and me may have been what is referred to as a contingent fee agreement; i.e., for one third or one fourth of the eventual recovery, if I am dismissed by you as your attorney I would not necessarily be entitled to that one third recovery but would be entitled to compensation for the reasonable value of the number of hours I devoted to the case.

Another type of lien that may arise is a tax lien. If you do not pay your property taxes for your real estate, then the local or state government may record a lien against your property. Likewise, if you do not pay your federal income or estate taxes, the federal government may file an IRS lien. Those liens are filed in the same office where the deed to your property is recorded and any attempt by you to sell the property will be impeded unless that lien is satisfied.

CONCLUSION

As you may have gathered from reading this book, I am very proud of being an attorney and how our legal system protects the rights of all people.

The legal profession is the protector of the unprotected, the advocate for unpopular causes and the spokesperson for those who cannot speak for themselves. Our Constitution and laws bestow upon each of us certain rights. The legal profession acts as a deterrent to those who might otherwise trample those rights and provides a vehicle for redress for those who have been injured by the unlawful or negligent acts of others. If lawyers did not zealously protect the rights of our citizens, then who else would? One need only look at the serious injuries caused by tobacco, breast implants, or prescription drugs to see that individuals and businesses are in fact accountable to us for injuries they cause by marketing and selling products that are not safe and that cause serious injuries, including death, to members of our society. Without the legal profession there would be no pressure on people and businesses to manufacture and sell safe products, build safe homes and cars, petition for laws to protect us in the workplace, overturn laws that are unfair, and prevent the government from taking our life, liberty or property without due process of law.

I hope that this book will provide you with a better understanding of our judicial system and will become a handy reference for you and your family to consult for many years to come.

About the Author

BRIEN A. ROCHE, ESQ.

Brien A. Roche is a 1976 graduate of the George Washington University School of Law and is a partner in the law firm of Johnson & Roche in McLean, Virginia. The focus of his law practice is civil litigation with an emphasis on medical malpractice, personal injury and wrongful death. Mr. Roche has extensive experience in all other aspects of civil litigation including contract, commercial, and domestic relations litigation and business advisory work.

Mr. Roche has taught law to students in a local college and is the noted author of two recognized legal texts: Virginia Torts Case Finder and the Virginia Domestic Relations Case Finder which are both published by the largest publisher of law books in the United States. In addition to his books, Mr. Roche is the author of articles that have appeared in The Journal of the Virginia Trial Lawyers Association, the Virginia Bar News and a publication disseminated by the Office of the Chief Medical Examiner of the Virginia State Department of Health. Mr. Roche has lectured at legal seminars on various topics including "Preparing and Trying An Automobile Personal Injury Case", "Tort Law Update" sponsored by the Virginia Trial Lawyers Association and a lecture on "Premises Liability" sponsored by the Virginia Association of Defense Attorneys.

In 1986, Mr. Roche was appointed and continues to serve as a Commissioner in Chancery for the Circuit Court of Fairfax County, Virginia.

Mr. Roche practices before Federal and State courts in Virginia, the District of Columbia and Maryland. He has argued successfully before the Virginia State Supreme Court, the U.S. Court of Appeals, and the D.C. Court of Appeals. Mr. Roche is a member of the Virginia State Bar, Maryland State Bar, District of Columbia Bar, Fairfax County Bar Association, District of Columbia Bar Association, Association of Trial Lawyers of America and Virginia Trial Lawyers Association.

In 1995, Mr. Roche founded American Legion Post 129

Baseball Team and has sponsored the team since its inception.

Brien Roche lives with his wife, Toni and seven children in Alexandria, Virginia.

www.ingramcontent.com/pod-product-compliance
Lightning Source LLC
Chambersburg PA
CBHW030943180526
45163CB00002B/681